How Being Consistent

Changed Everything

Jason DeZurik

Cover Art: Nathan Langert
Cover Photo: Darci and Kevin Burlew
Final Edit: Katie Erickson
Editors: Sara Benner, Katie Erickson, Jan Stoneburner

Printed in the United States of America

Worldview Warriors
P.O. Box 681
Findlay, OH 45839
www.worldviewwarriors.org

ISBN-13: 978-1467935012

ISBN-10: 1467935018

Rick,

Be Consistent!

Jeremiah 20:9

Dedicated to Jaya

*   *   *

The adventure continues

This is Part of The Story
of One Man and His Family's
Continuing Struggle
To Strive To Live God's Way
In Everything They Do

*For our **struggle is not against flesh** and blood,*
*but **against** the rulers, **against** the*
*authorities, **against** the powers of this dark world*
*and **against** the spiritual forces of evil in the*
heavenly realms.
Ephesians 6:12

Jason DeZurik

CONTENTS

ACKNOWLEDGEMENTS

Thank you:
Jesus Christ, Danny Castro, Pastor Derik Hines,
Pastor Chris Kneen, Pastor Nathan Buck,
Pastor Marc Quinter, Pastor Neal Whitney, Shane Adams,
Reggie McNeal, Scott Mason, Silverline, Ryan Edbreg,
Steve Adams, Andrew Raboin, New Vision FM,
Dan Kayser, Jon Bowlus, Bill Ramsey, Joe Emert,
Tentmakers Ministry, Tom and Shiloh Stimson,
Jerry and Lené Taylor, Bruce and Sue Feeney,
Milan and Connie Cramer, Laura Praske, Mike Rall,
Bill Seng, Logan Ames, Katie Erickson,
Max and Marilyn Picklesimer, Mark Larson,
Grant Schumacher, Jay and Brittany Sanders,
Charlie and Renee King, Mort, Patty and Mitch Rall,
Ridge and Associates, Larry Hoover, Gary Lieb,
Jerry and Lou Ann Murphy, John and Kris Joseph,
Frank and Judy DeZurik, Rebecca DeZurik,
Hanna Greenberg, all of Jaya's siblings,
The following congregations:
The Catalyst Church (Findlay, Ohio)
Trinity Evangelical Church (Upper Sandusky, Ohio)
North Branch United Methodist Church (Minnesota)
and so many other people that this would just go on
forever. You know who you are. Thank you.

Chapter 1

Leaving Security for Liberty

Give me liberty or give me death.
Patrick Henry

A pessimist sees the problems in every opportunity,
an optimist sees the opportunity in every problem.
Winston Churchill

[handwritten note: Pessimist: A person who tends to see the worst aspect of things or believe the worst will happen. Doubter, Doubting Thomas. Optimist: A person who tends to be hopeful + confident about the future or success of something.]

We live in an interesting time. The fact of the matter really is, though, that everyone has lived in interesting times. Whether it be new technological inventions, politically charged times, or through natural disasters. Every generation has its challenges. Every one.

The year of 2007 was quite a difficult year for my family and me. I was moving on from a position as a youth minister where I had been quite successful for almost ten years and had learned many things under some great men of God. The people there were wonderful and I learned a lot through good times and bad. It was a position that was very rewarding but I had also come to rely upon this position for a paycheck, to build friendships, and to have health insurance, among other benefits.

It was a very secure position and, at least on a human level, moving on seemed like a huge mistake. With a wife, five children, and number six on the way, this did not seem like the most opportune time to start a new career path. And with the looming bad economy and forecasts of it to surely get worse, I'm sure that it looked irresponsible, foolish, and impossible to many people.

God made it very clear about eight months earlier that it was time to move on. We were to start a new ministry, because the place where I was serving was taking a different direction than in the past. I knew I could no longer work under the leadership that had been put in place there.

I did want to move on, but I listened to the advice of those who were concerned not only for my family and me but looking out for themselves as well. I allowed these people, some who were well meaning and I realize now that some who were not well meaning, to influence me to stay on at this place longer than I should have. I must admit I was a bit hesitant though about this leap of faith that my family and I were about to make. Now that I know what I know today, I know I was hearing the voice of God clearly and did not immediately obey His leading. I allowed the fear I had of people influence my decisions back then instead of the fear, or what I will call the respect, of God to influence my decisions. Part of it was my own uncertainty about the future and whether or not I was hearing from God correctly. It was also difficult to leave the security I had in this wonderful position. So my wife of almost ten years, five children all under nine years of age at the time, and I had to deal with the insecurities that came along with completely stepping out in faith and trusting God. We also learned hard lessons of deciphering maturity in God's people and immaturity in them. This also was a time of great struggle realizing that some people who call themselves Christians really are not or at least appear to not be followers of Jesus Christ in and through their continuous sinful actions. In and through this time we grew greatly in our understanding of God being the Judge and that we are not the Judge. If you haven't sensed it yet, it was a very brutal time for my family and me. We didn't know it, at the time, but we would be heading down the narrow path Jesus Christ spoke of in Matthew 7. We would be trading in a stable and steady life for a life of uncertainty, much lower pay, and we would have to rethink how to live in a society where we wouldn't be the norm.

To put it bluntly, God basically said, "Do you trust me?" To which we said, "Yes." He responded with, "Then leave what you are comfortable with and follow me down the narrow path." We have had to rethink our whole approach to many things in this life.

The ministry we started is called Worldview Warriors and today it is even more than we thought it would be. God is using this ministry more throughout the world than I personally imagined up to this point. Worldview Warriors is now helping families in the Philippines get out of forced prostitution and slavery in our ministry partnership with Threads of Hope. Our Internet presence is being felt not only in North America, but also in Europe, Australia, Asia, and even Africa. God is moving through this ministry! Faces in the ministry have come and gone, but God continues to bring qualified, passionate people to the ministry for us to continue to raise the bar for Christ's Kingdom.

My family and I have been majorly stretched, refined, and pruned by God. He continues this process even today. This road has been very difficult, and at times, seemingly unbearable. My family and the team we have put together at Worldview Warriors continue to focus in on the Holy Spirit. We are learning more and more how to listen to the Spirit and be guided by the Spirit.

Since God has put my family and me on this Worldview Warriors journey, there have been plenty of times when we have wanted to say, "Enough—we're done!" However, God keeps showing us that this is not an option. We must stay the course and continue serving Him in this way. We are called to equip not only students and young adults, but anyone willing to learn what it means to become a fully devoted follower of Jesus Christ, even if it isn't comfortable or doesn't bring happiness. No matter what, we are all called to rejoice and fully rely on God for our needs as it says in Philippians 4:4-9:

> Rejoice in the Lord always. I will say it again: Rejoice! Let your gentleness be evident to all. The Lord is near. Do not be anxious about anything, but in everything,

by prayer and petition, with thanksgiving,
present your requests to God. And the
peace of God, which transcends all
understanding, will guard your hearts and
your minds in Christ Jesus.

Finally, brothers, whatever is true,
whatever is noble, whatever is right,
whatever is pure, whatever is lovely,
whatever is admirable — if anything is
excellent or praiseworthy — think about
such things. Whatever you have learned or
received or heard from me, or seen in me —
put it into practice. And the God of peace
will be with you.

One time in my life that this passage has been
demonstrated is by the following event that happened in
2009.

My family's favorite meal is breakfast, and we especially
love cereal, hot or cold. One morning my three-year-old
daughter, Eva, asked me for a bowl of "cerlo," my
daughter's word for cereal at the time. I retrieved the
bowls, spoons, and cereal and placed them all on the table.
As I poured the cereal, my daughter asked for "nilk." So I
went to the fridge to get the milk, but there was no milk in
the refrigerator. Next, I tried our beat-up, donated, second
fridge in the garage to get our extra milk. (With six kids,
we usually go through at least a gallon a day in our
house.) Much to my chagrin, that refrigerator was also

devoid of any milk.

So I went back inside the house and woke up my sleeping wife, Jaya, and told her that I'd be walking down to the grocery store to get some milk for our morning breakfast.

I was taken aback by her reply. She sat up quickly and said, "Oh no, you can't."

"Why not?" I asked.

She informed me that we had no cash.

I said, "Fine, I'll write a check."

She also informed me that we had no money in our checking account to write a check. We were broke!

Now I just want to be clear that we have no debt whatsoever and pay all our bills on time. Doing ministry is very challenging because there are times that it seems as if our needs will not be met. We do not at all live an extravagant lifestyle and often go without some basic necessities. But our needs are always met.

On this morning, however, I disregarded my wife's statement and said, "Yeah, whatever, I'm going to get some milk."

But she held fast, "No."

By this time our other children had begun to awaken because I was not being very quiet about this situation. I was very upset and, needless to say, the whole family knew I was not in a good mood.

Our whole family was now standing in the kitchen not knowing what to do, and then my wife looked at us and said, "Well, let's pray. Let's ask God to supply us some milk this morning."

I'm sure my face registered cynicism — "Are you joking?" — for my wife said, "Well, Daddy, you can just stay in here and have a bad attitude, but the kids and I are going to go into the dining room and pray."

And that is exactly what they did. My wife and six children sat down together at the dining room table, praying to the God of the universe, while I stood in the kitchen like a pouting child. I was not happy!

Then I heard my three-year-old daughter's small, soft voice say, "Dear Jesus, I like cerlo. We need some nilk. Please, Jesus, get us some nilk for our cerlo. We really like nilk." I couldn't hold back any longer. I started sobbing and joined my family.

About five minutes into our praying for "nilk," we heard a knock on the door. I was honestly startled and looked at my wife in shock. Surely, this couldn't be the milk we had been praying for, could it?

We opened the door to find our friend Christa standing in the doorway. She said, "Hey everyone, we're going on vacation to Minnesota for the next three weeks. We have some extra milk and don't want it to go bad. Do you need some milk?"

She held three gallons of milk in her hands.

With exclamation, we told her what had just happened, and we all rejoiced together about how God had heard our prayer and laid it on her heart to bring this over to us at that very moment.

There is no way this was just a coincidence. There is no way other than the prompting of the Holy Spirit that she knew to bring that to us. There is only one explanation and that is the God of the universe was looking over us and supplying our need in His way. We still praise God for this memorable display of His provision. In fact, He still supplies in this way a lot of times for our family.

Through this experience, we were able to truly live out the Philippians 4:4-9 passage I quoted before this story. We were able to rejoice in the fact that God provided for our need of milk. Yes, we would have been able to live through the day without milk, but God loves to bless His children and we were blessed to have our favorite meal of cereal that day. We asked God for milk by prayer and petition with thanksgiving as the passage commands us to do, and He truly provided. Even though I wasn't necessarily thinking about what is good and right during this experience, God used this to show me I needed to change my attitude to one of rejoicing instead of one of pouting. My entire family was able to put God's Word into practice in our daily lives – and enjoy our cereal as well.

Are you truly living out your faith in the real world? Are you actually hearing the voice of God and obeying Him or are you just saying that you are and then continuing to live the same old life you have lived year, after year, after year? Are you ready to live the full life and plan that God has for you and your family or just continue down the same broad path that you've been heading down? Only you can truly answer these questions.

Along with providing for my family's basic needs, another thing that was very difficult for us was leaving behind our health insurance for our soon-to-be family of eight in 2007. Our health insurance had previously cost over $14,000 a year. With my wife being four months pregnant, we were seriously concerned about how we would pay for this pregnancy, let alone deal with the expenses of a new baby. We could not afford a much cheaper health insurance plan, let alone this very expensive health insurance we had at the time. I tried to work something out with the lead pastor of the church along with the elder who dealt with staff matters like this about keeping my wife on the church health insurance coverage, but to no avail. After making what I thought was a fair presentation to my pastor and an elder of the church, the lead pastor paused and looked me right in the eye and said, "That's not going to happen." I will admit I was a bit taken a back and hurt. At the time I thought, "Almost ten years of service as a youth minister at a very successful ministry and this is how we are treated?"

I now realize this painful time in my life would be used for God and His glory. It would also be used in my marriage and our family for us to grow up and to stop being spiritual infants and adolescents in certain areas of our lives. It was a very hard time for my family and me. We were on our own with this issue and felt alone. Well, we were not actually alone, but we were on our own with God and some of our brothers and sisters in Christ from this church and community who continued to love us dearly. Our family still shows them love as well. We had to put our complete faith and trust in Christ that He would supply our needs and take care of us. Looking back on that time, we recognize that it was for our own good, but it can be hard to see the daylight when you are in the middle of a very long tunnel.

Now don't get me wrong; many, many people pray and help support our efforts for the Kingdom of God. Many of these wonderful brothers and sisters are from this amazing church family where I served as the youth minister for almost ten years. Many of these people continue to support our ministry to this day, but it's truly up to God to supply our needs.

Think about this: It's up to God to supply your needs.

Do you actually believe that?

God has been faithful in supplying our family's needs and
we have learned to go without in many ways. We have
learned more and more the difference between needs and
wants. God has supplied in many ways, from supplying
someone to pay completely for the pregnancy of our sixth
child (which you will soon read about), to shoes and
clothes and even board games for our children. He even
supplies us food like pork and beef just as we are about to
run out. Literally! God has supplied and continues to
supply our needs in and through His people and in
miraculous ways as well.

As I stated earlier, one of the most difficult decisions at the
time of leaving my stable youth ministry position was
what to do about health care for our family. I have
personally been ridiculed by Christians and non-Christians
alike for what I am about to tell you.

My wife and I had been trained, probably a lot like you
are, that we needed and deserved health insurance.
Especially since at the time we had a family of seven
people. We definitely didn't have the money to pay for
COBRA, which we could have gotten for a time to have
some "peace of mind." It was far too expensive for our
income. So, we went without health insurance for about a
month.

As you already know, at this time my wife was pregnant
with our sixth child and she was due in October of 2007.

We definitely needed health insurance for her pregnancy, or so we thought. We even went through the hoops and paperwork to get the government health insurance that was and remains available for people, but we knew deep down that it was a mistake. We knew God was not calling us to use this government service. It was a difficult time for us because we had unknowingly been trained to think inside of this man-made system. Not having health insurance at the time seemed like utter foolishness. We had been trained to trust in human ideas and not in God and His ways of wisdom. God was calling us to obey Him and trust Him. So, we cancelled the government insurance and relied on God. This was about six to eight weeks before our daughter was born.

About one month before our daughter was about to grace us with her presence, someone contacted us, stopped over, and told us these words, "My husband and I have been praying and if we don't pay for this pregnancy, God has told us we would be sinning." My wife and I were shocked, dumb-founded, and amazed! We hadn't told anyone of our need and yet this woman of God was telling us that God had told her that they needed to pay completely for this pregnancy. This included all doctor visits before the birth, the birth itself, and any check ups with the midwife right after the birth.

God spoke to this couple about our situation. They heard Him and obeyed. Even though it was hard not to have health insurance, God blessed us immensely for our trust in Him. He is our Provider.

Are you willing to admit that God is your Provider?

Are you willing to completely trust in God?

Are you willing to trust the God who gives you life?

I know it took a while for us to understand this and actually do this but it is very rewarding.

And that's not the end of the story! Having a baby can cost anywhere between $3,000 – $10,000 or more. Yet, when we received the bill from the local hospital for the delivery of our baby girl the bill came to only $1,000. That was it! Not only did God supply our need, but He blessed the couple who paid for this entire pregnancy as well with a bill far below what we were expecting. My wife even called the hospital to make sure there wasn't any mistake and sure enough there was no mistake. God is so good.

I don't care where you are at in your walk with God. HE LOVES YOU! If you think He does not exist, HE LOVES YOU! He made you and knows how you work. If you are totally sold out to Him, HE LOVES YOU! He loves you so much that you can choose to follow Him or deny Him. One thing is for sure, He wants the best for you. One question you need to ask yourself is, "Am I willing to hear God's voice and obey no matter what the cost?" I implore you to answer that question with a huge "Yes!!!!" You will not be sorry.

So began my family's journey from security to liberty. We

began to truly live out God's ways in the world consistently. We were living out the Kingdom of God in all our ways. We were learning to hear God's voice and obey His leading. The Kingdom of God is not heaven. It is not a program. It is not an institution set up by humans. It is a mind-set. It is a spiritual awakening. It is a lifestyle.

For us, hearing and obeying God took us to a very interesting place. We learned to grow and realize that we are responsible for our actions, and that blaming others is acting like a child. Hebrews 5:11–14 can help explain this idea. It says:

> We have much to say about this, but it is hard to explain because you are slow to learn. In fact, though by this time you ought to be teachers, you need someone to teach you the elementary truths of God's word all over again. You need milk, not solid food! Anyone who lives on milk, being still an infant, is not acquainted with the teaching about righteousness. But solid food is for the mature, who by constant use have trained themselves to distinguish good from evil.

We need to stop acting like a child with our actions of blaming others for the outcomes of things but we also need to have a child like faith in trusting in God to supply our needs. This can be difficult to understand but I hope in and through this book you will begin to understand even more.

How are you and your family doing following the narrow

14

path put in front of you by God? I encourage you to not only go through the narrow gate but start living the narrow path as well that Jesus discussed in Matthew 7:13-23. But I will warn you: it is not an easy path.

*　　*　　*

Are you dealing with anything difficult in your life right now? If you are, write it down and ask the Lord to guide you through this.

- Finances
- Debt
- Faith / Trust
- Marriage
- My weight + self Love
- Mothering to Isabel

LoRd,
Please guide
me through. →

↓ Amen

Supply my every need, LoRd. And also my families needs.
Amen

Matthew 7:13 says, Enter by the narrow gate...

Because narrow is the gate + difficult is the way which leads to life, and there are few who find it.
(Matthew 7:14)

Broad: Wide
Narrow: Not wide.

Jason DeZurik

*   *   *

In the United States of America, many of us seem
to be moving from a mindset of liberty to slavery,
and many of us don't even know it.
In fact, many seem to be welcoming it.

*   *   *

Jason DeZurik

Chapter 2

God Supplies Our Needs

Do not worry about your life. ✳
Jesus Christ

(Advice, guidance, direction.)

Never take counsel of your fears.
The enemy is more worried than you are.
General George S. Patton Jr.

$\mathcal{M}$y family and I have really taken those words of Jesus
to heart, to not worry about your life. You see, we used to
trust in human ways and we didn't even know it. Now we
truly trust in God and His ways. Here's the incredible
thing we have learned and realized: God wants to work in
and through His people in order to make Himself known.
Yes, He could do it without us, but it seems as if He
doesn't want to. God wants His people to hear His voice
and obey. In doing so, people who are not followers of
Jesus will be more open to the Holy Spirit as they see the
Spirit work in and through our lives.

Do you really believe that God supplies your needs? Most
of us that call ourselves Christ followers know what the
Bible says about this, but do we really believe this to be

19

true? Or do we actually worry about most things, not relying on God to supply? If each one of us would take a hard honest look at ourselves, I think we can admit that we are usually putting our faith and trust in humans to supply our needs. Some of us may even be putting our faith and trust in the provision and not the Provider. Yes, I am writing to you. You take a good look at yourself. Not your neighbor. Not your brother or sister. Ask God to help you look at you. *My God is the Provider of All things, + I know He will take care of my every need. Trust in the Provider not the providing.*

As you read through each one of these true stories, know that it has taken my wife and me years to get to this point of trusting in God, and we surely have not arrived yet. We daily check ourselves, and remind ourselves that we need to trust Him and rely on Him daily.

You will read more in chapter five about our continued journey into leaning on God and His people regarding family health care but before we get to that I want to share how God supplies in so many other ways too.

For instance, one week before we were going to make a very long trip to Minnesota for ministry and for our annual family reunion, we had no vehicle to take us. In 2011, our twelve passenger van basically was beyond repair. We didn't know how we were going to make it out there. So we prayed and asked God that He would supply us a vehicle for this trip if He wanted us to go. Of course, being a man and an American, I took matters into my own hands by going to dealerships and looking for anything that might work for us. Everything was way too expensive so I quit looking for a vehicle and just trusted in God.

A friend of mine had an eight-passenger van, but he was on vacation in Arkansas. Borrowing his van seemed out of the question at the time, but as it turned out, he was already on his way home and that van became an option for my family and me. In fact, my friend even got it road worthy for us after his long trip. He let us borrow it for three weeks while we were in Minnesota. Here's where the story gets interesting.

On the way to Minnesota, his van started acting up a bit while we were driving through Wisconsin. Since I was unfamiliar with the vehicle I just thought maybe that was typical of it from time to time. Our twelve passenger van that was not worth fixing had to have the transmission replaced; little did we realize that the transmission on this van we had just borrowed was about to have some serious issues too. It started shifting very hard, and I figured out that the transmission was the problem. The Lord had us stop at a great transmission shop in Buffalo, MN, which was owned by a Christian man. He said, "This could be a relatively inexpensive repair of approximately $800, or you might need a new transmission."

My first thought was, "Seriously, Lord?! Another transmission?" So, I called the van's owner to let him know the details, and he decided to try the cheaper repair since the other repair was in the thousands of dollars.

Well, the cheaper repair worked. Praise God! After three weeks we were on our way home as a family after our time in Minnesota.

After being in Ohio for about two days after our vacation, the owner of the van asked me what my wife and I thought of the van. I told him we really liked the van and might be interested in buying it if he wanted to sell it. He said, "We need to get together tonight if that's okay with you and your wife."

So, we met at a local restaurant in Upper Sandusky, Ohio to discuss the terms of a sale of the van. After talking a bit about our trip to Minnesota and getting to know each other better, they asked my wife and me what we thought of the van. My wife told them how much she liked it and how much she would love to purchase it but didn't know how we would pay for it.

The owner then asked his wife if she wanted to tell us how much they wanted to sell it to us for and she said, "Since you like the van so much, we have talked and we would like to sell you the van for . . . [she paused here] one dollar." They informed us that God had told them to sell us the van.

My wife immediately started to tear up and covered her mouth with her hands in shock. Heck, I was shocked! So that is how we bought a van for one dollar. You see, God wants to use His people. We need to be wiling to hear God's voice and obey. This advice applies to the giver of the gift and the person receiving the gift as well.

In the summer of 2012, my family and I were once again planning to go to Minnesota to do some ministry at a large Christian music festival and then go to our family reunion.

In March I had to make a decision if we would head to the music festival or not because I needed to pay for our booth space in advance. Trusting in God to supply our needs, but not knowing if we would have the funds in the future or not, I decided to get the booth space, pay for it in March, and believe the rest of the funds would come in for our trip later in the year.

One week before we were preparing to leave for Minnesota, we did not have the funds to make this trip. In fact, we were approximately $2200 short, which also included bills that needed to be paid on top of expenses of going to Minnesota. Knowing what had happened in the past and learning from it, my wife and I just trusted in God to supply our needs. We were leaving on a Monday for Minnesota, and we started praying for God to supply our need on the Monday before we were leaving. The reality is, we were planning to leave at 4:00 in the morning on that Monday, so if the Lord was to supply our need through a check we needed this money no later than Saturday morning, but I was hoping for Friday evening.

We prayed Monday for the Lord to supply our need and presented our request like this: "Lord, we know you are the owner of everything and know that this financial need for you is no problem. We do have a financial need of $2,200 that needs to be supplied by next Monday, and we believe already that you have supplied it. We thank you for supplying our needs. Thank you for being such a good God and Father. In Jesus' name we pray, amen."

That was the gist of it and we left it at that. In the past I had been worried about these sorts of things, but not this time. I knew God would supply our needs because He had done it so many times in the past. *Just because we worry, doesn't mean He won't supply. But, He tells us to not worry.*

Well, no money came in on Monday. Tuesday rolled around and my wife and I continued to pray, but nothing financially happened. Wednesday was July 4th. We prayed again in the morning, but still nothing happened. Thursday came and went. We prayed as usual, but no financial blessing of $2,200 came in. We did receive about $100 from faithful supporters of the ministry, and we thank God for that; but it was not the $2,200 we were waiting and praying for. Friday morning came; Jaya and I prayed again. I was genuinely not worried. In the past I had let my emotions and lack of faith get the best of me but this time was different. Why? I completely put my faith and trust in the Lord. I knew He would supply.

Here's a little tidbit I find interesting. I think it is very important to this story and the importance of having a marriage built upon the Lord. In the past Jaya has been the one who would encourage me when I would get down or have lack of faith that God would supply. In this way she helped strengthen not only my walk with God but also our marriage and family in the process. This time around, my wife made the comment, "I know God will supply, but what if it doesn't come by Monday? What are we going to do?"

I replied, "Don't worry. God will supply today or tomorrow I am not concerned about this at all."

You see what happened there?

Because of my wife's faith in the past she helped me grow in my faith, and so today when she lacks faith I am able to encourage her. Many times it's my wife encouraging me in my faith. She is such an amazing woman of God!

So, I went to work on that Friday and left this situation regarding the money we needed for our trip in the hands of God. He was the one in charge of this, not me. It is so freeing when you realize that it really is all God's responsibility, and we just have to obey His leading.

When I got home that evening, my wife was a little teary and pulled out a check that someone had given her. It was for $1,200. Then I pulled out a check for $1,000 that I had received that afternoon. We praised God and thanked Him for His provision and faithfulness of giving us $2,200 in and through His people who obeyed His leading. We were going to be able to make this trip with no worries at all. Now let me be clear; we had told no one of this need except for God. We did not go out and ask for these funds from people. This was people hearing the voice of God and obeying His leading.

Still other times, people will just drop by with beef or pork or fresh produce for our family, not knowing that we had just run out or were about to run out. We have also seen God work in allowing us to give in this way as well to those in need.

Here is one more example of how God has supplied our needs. My wife is an excellent writer and always tries to write a memorable Christmas letter. She always writes a little about each member of the family. So, one year in our Christmas letter, she wrote about two of our daughters who were playing the board game Candy Land. In our home, this game had already been through four other children. She described how one of the pieces to mark your spot was from another game and it was basically falling apart and how the other piece was a chewed up piece of foam that was in the shape of a triangle. It was pretty funny at the time and it still is funny. That year was something special. Let's just say that God's people showed up!

After being gone all day one day, we came home to a box on our porch. It was full of all these things my wife had written about in the Christmas letter. Soccer balls, sleds and yes, even a Candy Land game. To this day we still have no idea who gave us everything in that box. It was amazing and it was such a wonderful gift to receive. What is awesome is that we knew this was one way God was showing He loved us. He wasn't done there though. Someone else showed up to our house with a bunch of games, which included, you guessed it, Candy Land. God wasn't done working in and through His people there though either. One more Candy Land game showed up at our house very soon after that as well. It was incredible to know God loves us, even through a simple game like Candy Land.

We have had similar experiences in giving as well. For

instance, we are blessed to be able to support an orphanage in India, and from time to time we will send funds to the person in charge of this orphanage. Many times we send an amount that we believe the Lord has put on our heart to send. Many times we will get a note back that says, "Praise the Lord brother Jason and sister Jaya! The money you sent was the exact amount I had just prayed for God to supply. What a blessing!"

Friends, all Christ-followers must start acting like the church of Jesus Christ. We need to start helping people on an individual basis and through the church. As we have all seen, many government organizations try to do a good job but often fall flat on their faces because of red tape, regulations, and rules that many times do nothing but hinder them from doing good. There are a lot of wasted finances that could be dealt with and given away so much easier through each individual and the church.

When individual believers actually decide to follow what is taught in God's word and individually help the poor and widows, we might actually see some change in the world. We should help through our local congregations as well. We need to stop giving to the world and government what God has called us to do, and what He has instituted, (like the gift of marriage between one man and one woman) so that Christ's church may actually rise up and become relevant in the world again. Let me be very clear. I am discussing the entire body of Christ, not just your local congregation. I am discussing the Church as a whole. There are many church programs and things the church does that are good and we should not take away from those. However, it seems that many, though not all, Christ followers have taken the easy way out and give toward things while others do the work. Are funds needed? Absolutely! But so are workers. In my humble opinion, until we as individual Christ followers start taking responsibility for what we are called to do as individuals in the body of Christ to further Christ's Kingdom, we will only see more of the same: a sick Church limping along, losing ground to the world that needs healing. If you think I am off base I would ask you to pray and seek out God's leading on this statement.

*   *   *

For further study:
Acts 2:42-47 If we as followers of Christ put this example of the early church into action today we might actually become relevant in the world again without becoming like the world.

Matthew 9:36-38 As followers of Christ it is clear that God is calling us to go and do.

The church must start working together and stop bickering and fighting amongst ourselves. It is clear we need to work together as it promotes in Ecclesiastes 4:11-12.

When we are consistent and put Scriptures like these into practice, things begin to be revealed to us, especially how we are a part of God's plan. When we as individual

followers of Christ make Him the center of everything is when each one of us will begin to see results in our lives as well as the lives of others.

Dear Lord,

Help me to make You the center of everything in my life. I want to see change + You working things out for my good + my families good. What is Your plan for my life? Help me to stay consistent in Your Word + with prayer so that I will know what You want from me. Help me to not worry about my life. Help me to put my trust in You, the Provider of All, + not in the providing. Help me to hide Your Word in my heart so that I may know what You want from me. I want to be so much like You, that others see You through me.

In Jesus name,

Amen

Jason DeZurik

Chapter 3

It's a Lifestyle

We can't have two sets of standards, one set for the dedicated young men who want to do something ambitious and one set for those who don't.
Bear Bryant

If we find ourselves with a desire that nothing in this world can satisfy, the most probable explanation is that we were made for another world.
C.S. Lewis

Have we become so carnal, self-absorbed, and self-centered that we don't even see the truth anymore? Have we as believers in Jesus Christ allowed the world and its ways to influence us more than we've influenced it? Unfortunately, it seems the answer is, "yes."

Black Friday, the shopping day after Thanksgiving, is a perfect example of the blind carnality and self-absorption that many of us have. Many of us see the videos posted on the Internet of people scrambling for things like cell phones, the toy of the year, and so on and I have to wonder: Has it really come to this? A Christian friend of mine told me that on Black Friday, he jumped for one of the three remaining laptops for the sale price of $299. (Ok, I probably would have done the same thing, but does this attitude glorify Christ?) The entertainment industry wades in the desire of Christians and non-Christians alike to escape from reality through entertainment. For instance, game companies now flood the market with board games about television shows. In addition, instead of actually playing tennis, bowling, or exercising, we now play a sport on our video game console and equate it with the real thing. Rather than getting only a regular size soda, we order what seems to be a keg of soda just for one sitting, and we presume that is normal.

Here's more proof: My father and I were in a fast food restaurant one day to purchase two chicken sandwiches, a small fry, and two small drinks for us for lunch. The man behind him handed the cashier a coupon for a chicken sandwich and told her, "They usually let me get three with this." Let me tell you that this man certainly was not in need of three sandwiches, if you know what I mean. However, since he was with a couple of people, we supposed that the sandwiches were for them. After the cashier's approval, the man pulled out three more coupons for three sandwiches each, for a grand total of twelve sandwiches, and ordered fries, drinks, etc. Thus, the three of them sat down to devour their feast.

Some of you might be thinking, "What's the big deal? They had the money, and the restaurant approved it. So why write about that?" Despite the obvious fact that such a habit is unhealthy, here's the truth that I am trying to convey for you to ponder: Have we, as the Church, gotten so complacent that we just want to be entertained and spoon-fed from the pulpit? For those of you in small churches, have you become numb to winning people to Christ or so focused on your "club" that you think that infant baptism and confirmation are enough to be a Christian? You may go to church services every Sunday morning just to get your spiritual charge for the week, to gorge yourself on the biblical message to last you until next week.

But do you care to live your faith during the week?

Do you want to live or just survive?

We need to realize that God has so much more for us than just survival in the life that He has given us. Some of you in large churches also need to be aware of your attitude toward church. In a busy, active church, it is easy to get lost in Sunday morning services and programs that fill your time throughout the week and forget that there is so much more to the Christian life. I know because I've lived it.

Live the life that God has called you to live! Get into ministry opportunities right where you are. But don't contain "ministry" to just within the walls of your church building. Go out into the world, as the disciples did after Jesus went home to heaven. They were merely following His example; He ministered right where He was in the everyday world. Don't remain locked away in some church craft club, church athletic program or a cliquey Sunday school class. When Jesus went to the temple, He questioned the status quo and seemed to challenge the hypocrisy that the institution had become. Jesus did not challenge God and His ways, but He challenged the man-made, man-instituted rules that the religious leaders of the day were placing upon the people. Perhaps it is time to follow Christ's example. He did not challenge people and their practices to be a jerk or a problem. I believe He genuinely wanted people to search for the truth.

✳ What about you? Are you tired of the mundane and the table scraps you are receiving? My real adventure began once I woke up from my slumber, realized how I had become conditioned to just get by, and I finally made a conscious decision to hear God's voice and obey no matter what. Do you feel like you're just surviving? Your needs and your wants are being met, but are you truly living? Are you living the adventure that God has in store for you? Maybe living for God has become just a religion or a list of rules to fulfill your obligations to the Supreme Being and others. If it does, you might need to reevaluate your relationship with God. ✳

Is the Church as we know it really the way that it is supposed to be? Is the corporate and business-like institution that it has become of God or of men? Is this really the church that Jesus envisioned? These musings do not necessarily apply to all congregations. I am merely referring to the institutional methods that many churches push and how many Christians (including myself) have gotten caught up in these models. I may or may not be addressing your situation; you know if this applies to you.

Back when I was a young, naïve youth worker, I used to believe that I was essentially a pastor to students and their families. They seemed to agree, for I would perform "pastoral duties," and the families did not object. My senior pastor at the time stressed that since I was considered a pastor, I should use my God-given gifts accordingly. I was hesitant at first because of my respect for the church and what it represents, but I gradually became comfortable with the idea due to the ministry that was happening in the community. Thus, many ordained pastors and I considered myself a pastor. As I was encouraged, I continued to try to use my gifts in a positive way for the Kingdom of God.

However, my world was rocked in 2006; well, it was more like a major earthquake. Another senior pastor told me that I was not a pastor and was not even considered one, even though I was already performing pastoral duties. Confused, I asked why he believed this. He stated that since I had not received seminary training and was not ordained, I was not a pastor. (I am not bashing a seminary education. I am sure that it is fine teaching.)

He then informed me I was not qualified to baptize anyone or bless communion, even though I had already been doing so for several years. I asked him for an explanation of why I needed to be ordained. He simply stated that it was the church's requirement. I wondered where this teaching is found in the Bible.

I wondered aloud, "Were Phillip and Peter ordained? They both baptized people." He gave no reply, so I moved forward.

"Was John ordained? He certainly baptized and offered communion." Once again, his reply was silence. I pressed on.

"And for that matter, was Jesus ordained?" Now he had an answer for me: "Well, He's God. And the disciples were with Jesus, so it was acceptable for them."

"What?!" I said. (I was thinking, "Are those words really coming out of your mouth?") I continued, "I have a conversation with God everyday!"

Now, I am not trying to start a battle or divisions within the church, but let's consider this: What is the Church? Is it Sunday morning in a building, singing a few songs and listening to the "professionals" sharing their wisdom? Or is it the Church, the body of Christ, living every day to bring glory to Christ in all that we do? The Church is every day, everywhere we are, not just in a building. I believe Acts 2:42-47, is an example of what the Church is supposed to look like: ✳

> They devoted themselves to the apostles'
> teaching and to the fellowship, to the
> breaking of bread and to prayer. Everyone
> was filled with awe, and many wonders
> and miraculous signs were done by the

apostles. All the believers were together and had everything in common. Selling their possessions and goods, they gave to anyone as he had need. Every day they continued to meet together in the temple courts. They broke bread in their homes and ate together with glad and sincere hearts, praising God and enjoying the favor of all the people. And the Lord added to their number daily those who were being saved.

I almost let the institution change who I am in Christ. I almost let it tame me, as I began to fall into the mundane and the status quo and the cliques. But praise God — He woke me up from this stupor of normalcy to face reality.

My wife and I are excited because we believe that the truth is slowly coming out. It has been a long, hard road, which may only get more difficult. However, God does not call us as Christians to a comfortable life.

Doing ministry outside of the norm of the institution of the church has been exciting, difficult, and crazy at times. But no matter what, we are committed to completing this journey. We believe that we have been called to a ministry of lifting up the body of Christ and, when necessary, helping members of the body tackle the difficult issues. I believe these are just two of the aspects of the purpose of the body of Christ, the Church.

Know that all of us that are a part of the ministry of Worldview Warriors are here for you. We not only have speaking engagements and events all across the country for you to attend but we have been blessed by God to run an online community that you can be a part of right now. You can find out how, by getting started at www.worldviewwarriors.org. We also run a few radio programs where you can interact with us. More importantly, God is here for you as we all walk this journey of the Christian life He has called each one of us to.

Church, let's become the Church of Christ that we have been called to be. We are not building an institution or a program. It is a mind-set. It is a spiritual awakening. It is a lifestyle!

Are you ready to live for Christ with a reckless abandon, not worrying about yourself or what others think about you? I know my family and I are, and we want to welcome you to join us in this adventure for Christ. Live the adventure of a lifetime serving Christ where you are, no matter where that is and no matter your circumstances.

If you believe that I am out of line, please let me know. I am easily reachable on Facebook and you can contact me through our Worldview Warriors website found at www.worldviewwarriors.org. You will find out very quickly that one of our main purposes is discussing things with truth in love. We can discuss issues with gentleness and respect, as I Peter 3:15-16 encourages us. Whether you agree or disagree with me, I would love to hear from you. Let me stress that whether or not you agree with my musings, my desire is to pursue the truth and expose any falsehood so we can better serve Christ.

Let me close this chapter with one more thought. Over the years, I have been in dialogue with many pastors over the "church" issue and the pastoral issue. Surprisingly, many of them agree with my assessment of the situation but are afraid to speak up for fear of losing their credentials and retirement. Ladies and gentlemen, fear God and not man!

*   *   *

Here is some further reading for your consideration:

Acts 2 especially verses 42–47

Acts 3 Are you witnessing in the streets? We are called to it.

Matthew 28:18–20

I Corinthians 6:1–8 Something to think about. Is it okay to be wronged and to keep your mouth shut when you know you are right about something but leadership has a different mindset? The truth will eventually come out.

Matthew 5, 6, and 7.

<u>1 Peter 3:15</u>

Jason DeZurik

But <u>Sanctify</u> the Lord God in your hearts,

→

(
Purify
cleanse
Make Holy
Set apart
)

and always be ready to give

a <u>defense</u> to everyone who

↓

Asks you a reason
for the hope that
is in you. With

<u>Meekness</u> + <u>fear</u>;

↓   ↓

gentleness   Respect
Submissiveness

<u>1 Peter 3:16</u>

having a good <u>conscience</u>, that when

↓

moral
sense.
values.
inner feeling or voice,
acting as a guide to right + wrong

they <u>defame</u> you as evildoers, those who revile

↓

(
damage the
good reputation
of someone.
slander
)

Your good <u>conduct</u>   in Christ may

↓

(
manner in
which a person
behaves.
behavior.
Actions.
)

be <u>ashamed</u>.

↓

(
Embarrassed
guilty
sorry
)

(
criticize
in a
Abusive
or
angrily
manner.
Attack.
)

*   *   *

Our basic plan of operation is to advance and to keep on advancing regardless of whether we have to go over, under, or through the enemy.
General George S. Patton Jr.

*   *   *

Jason DeZurik

Chapter 4

Miracles and Demons

Any time you have an opportunity to make a difference in this world and you don't, then you are wasting your time on earth.
Roberto Clemente

My kingdom is not of this world. If it were, my servants would fight to prevent my arrest by the Jews. But now my kingdom is from another place.
Jesus Christ / John 18:36

In 2004 so much changed in my world of youth ministry, but I wouldn't come to realize much of it until 2006, as at times, unfortunately, I can be a slow learner. My beliefs in the church, the Bible, and even who I believed God was were seriously challenged. Much of my confusion came because of beliefs of others who I respected. I soon came to realize, though, that some of these people were still infants in their faith in Christ even though they had been put in a high position within the church.

It's not that I really didn't believe in miracles or in demonic activity, but some people had told me that these things were not for today. Others did tell me they were for

43

today, but said we didn't see God work in this way much anymore. I just had never really experienced these sorts of things before, only in a very small way but that was about it.

Today, I see that God had been training up my family and me to become more mature in Him. Sometimes He does this through hardship and adversity and other times He allows rest but it is to grow in the Kingdom of God. God was growing in us an even greater spiritual awareness of how He wants to use people to further His plan in and through the way, the truth, and the life of Jesus Christ. Much of this journey began in 1994 and you will read about some of it in chapter nine. The Lord led my wife, Jaya, and me to move to Ohio in 1997 to help continue a youth ministry at a growing church in Upper Sandusky. We were open to God's direction and obeyed Him. This was a vital training time for me in becoming a disciple of Christ that I will need to discuss another time in great length. That time was an amazing time of spiritual maturity for my whole family, but I realized in 2006 that God was calling us to something even greater. In fact, God orchestrated our exit from there as you've already read about, but there is so much more to that story. Hopefully, I can share that with you another time.

In 2007 I left my comfortable youth ministry position to pursue what I believed to be God's plan for the life of me and my family. Little did I realize how difficult that would be. Starting a new ministry completely from scratch is far more difficult than anyone can imagine unless you have tried it yourself. When we started Worldview Warriors, there were three founding members to the ministry: two good friends of mine that I had known for many years, and me. In about two years I was the only one left as my two friends had decided to move on to other endeavors. Continuing on the path God has called you to can be even more difficult if you do not recognize that we are in a spiritual battle every day of our lives. If you make a choice to follow God's plan for your life it means you will be serving God right where He wants you and you'll be exactly where Satan and his demons won't want you to be, so it can be difficult at times to persevere through the continual adversity. When you know God is calling you to do something, you need to obey His leading because He will lead you to His plan. That's the real adventure that He already has planned for you. It isn't easy, but it is the best plan for you because God put it together.

After two years of the Worldview Warriors ministry being in existence, I was the only founding member left. Man, was that difficult! I had to put a new board in place and once that came together we knew that we needed to continue down the path of our mission statement, "Equipping Students to Impact This Generation for Jesus Christ." With that, I set out on the road doing events all across the country. In two years I had traveled to over twenty states.

The beginning of 2009 was quite an eye opener for me. In March, I was able to go out on the road with a band I had met just two years earlier at the Sonshine Music Festival in Willmar, MN. Little did I realize what a huge blessing this would be in my life. The band's name was Silverline. I had no idea what we were about to encounter and experience on our two-week trip throughout the southwestern United States.

We were blessed to do a "Spiritual Emphasis Week" at a Christian school in Texas with not only Silverline and myself but also with many speakers from the ministry of Worldview Warriors. It was an honor to be allowed to teach and speak not only into the lives of the students at this school but also into the teachers and staff as well. The first day just went wonderfully. Yes, we had some "hitches" technically, but that's to be expected. Something that took place that day would change the scope of the ministry of Worldview Warriors and also how I personally would move more toward pleasing God and not humans. I didn't realize yet how I would begin seeking out God's will and plan even if it didn't fit into my "God box." By my "God box" I mean how people try to put God in a box and think how God should work or should be working in the world today. Yet, when some people experience a working of the Holy Spirit in a way they cannot understand (their "God box") they either ignore it or explain it away. I am not bashing anyone here at all, in fact I used to be like this in many ways.

The entire time at the school was seriously amazing! We were open to and obeyed the leading of the Holy Spirit. Let me provide an example. During lunch at the school one day, I noticed Ryan Edberg, the lead singer of Silverline, running across the school courtyard all by himself. It was more like running and jumping all by himself. Picture if you will a ballerina performing a graceful run and jump over and over. Now picture a grown man doing the same thing without the graceful part, and that's kind of what Ryan looked like. I could tell he was excited about something. He ran over to me and in a excited, frantic, and joyous tone Ryan proceeded to tell me, near as I can remember, the following story:

"Yesterday, a girl came up to me and asked me if we really believed the things we are teaching them in the workshops. I told her, of course; why do you ask me that? She said, 'Even the healing parts? Do you believe that God can heal people today?'

"I said, 'Of course.'

"She told me that she had a bad back for the last six years, and in her sixth grade year she needed to quit volleyball and all sports because of it. She could not bend well at all and her back obviously affected her even to this day.

"So, she asked me to pray for God to heal her back. I laid hands on her back and prayed for God to heal her. Today she came up to me all excited and said, 'Look at this! I'm healed! God healed me!' And she could bend back and forth and side to side with no problems."

Ryan was so excited he was like a little boy. I was pretty excited also, but a bit skeptical. So, I went to the superintendent of the school. Why? If this girl was lying and just making up this story surely he could help me get to the bottom of this.

I went to him and just shot the breeze for a bit and asked him if he was enjoying the week and he said, "Yes." I said something like thanks and praise God and then I asked him if he knew who this girl was. It worked out perfectly because she had walked into the room we were in and was easily identified, as she was blonde and was wearing a bright blue shirt.

I asked him, "Do you know that girl over there with the blonde hair and blue shirt?" He said, "Yes, we know each other very well." Just before I was about to ask him about this girl's back he interrupted me and said, "How is she doing that?"

I replied, "Doing what?"

He said, "She's had a bad back for about six years now and had to quit volleyball and basketball because of it. How is she doing that?"

I said, "What do you mean?"

He said, "She should not be bending like that."

Well, I had my confirmation! This was in fact a healing from God. It was legit. So I shared what had happened the day before with Ryan and the superintendent of the school clearly did not know what to make of it. Even though he could see that she was clearly healed, he still seemed skeptical.

One thing that was clear though is that the students were not skeptical. One student came up to me, hit me in the shoulder, and said, "You guys believe in healing?"

I said, "Yes, we believe all of the Bible is true."

She looked me right in the eye, with her friends all around her and said, "Then why didn't you pray for my healing yesterday when I told you I was deaf in my one ear since I was six years old?" Honestly, I really didn't know what to say because it was at that moment that I realized that maybe I was hindering people coming to the Lord with my lack of belief.

So, the students around her and I laid hands on her and prayed over her. I asked in Jesus name for the Lord to heal her. When I was done praying, she said, "Whisper in my ear." I did and she started jumping up and down and running around in a circle exclaiming, "I'm healed, I'm healed. I can hear! I can hear!" Even though I had just witnessed this, I was so shocked and dumbfounded that God would want to work in and through me to heal this girl. It was so amazing and awesome that Silverline and I left that school in awe of what God had just done. We all wondered, what would happen next?

A few days later we were in California. After I had spoken and Silverline had played, many people came up and talked to us about many things. One young man in particular, who was seventeen years old at the time, came up to me and made some pretty interesting comments. I will call him "Joe" in this recollection of what took place.

"That was a very interesting talk," Joe said.

I said, "Praise God and thank you very much I really appreciate that."

Joe replied, "You really make the Greek and Hebrew come alive! I have never really looked at it that way before."

"Really?" I said. "You know Greek and Hebrew?"

"Yes, I can read both and what you said really came to life." Joe said.

At this point I was a little hesitant because this young man was only seventeen years old. How could he know Greek and Hebrew? But we continued our conversation.

"I'm hoping you can help me out," Joe said.
I asked, "How so?"

"I hear voices in my head."

"What kind of voices?" I replied.

"Just voices. I have been to four different university hospitals for help and so far not one of them has been able to cure these voices in my head. I am on medication but it doesn't really help."

At this point, I was thinking maybe this young man was telling me a tall tale or was schizophrenic or possibly had some other mental illness. I just wasn't sure what to say or do so I listened to him for quite a while. I asked Andrew Raboin, Silverline's keyboardist at the time, and our roadie to listen in and join in praying for this young man, as I wasn't really sure what to make of this situation. So after listening to this young man tell his story, I suggested that we pray for him. To be brutally honest, I was just figuring we would pray over this young man and then move on to talk with someone else; but a different plan was definitely in the making. I put my right hand on this young man's left shoulder and put my left hand on this young man's chest and began to pray. I prayed for him as a man and for his relationship with God to grow and mature, but I knew I needed to get to "it." But what was "it"? "It" was to proclaim that this young man be healed or delivered from demon possession in the name of Jesus Christ.

I knew this because in Scripture we read that people are delivered in the name of Jesus, and we had just experienced healings happen in Texas in the name of Jesus Christ.

So, I finished up my prayer with the following words, "And if there are any demons in or around Joe right now, we command you to leave Joe and go back to the pit of hell where you belong. We command you to do this in the name of Jes . . ." And that is all the farther I got. I was about to say, "Jesus Christ." This young man stayed standing, but his arms moved up and his hands moved like claws. He hissed at us like an animal or like a lizard, and his head cocked back a bit. He also was slightly lunging forward with his head as if to bite me with his mouth.

I jumped back as this happened, and Andrew, along with the roadie, began to speak in another language that I could not understand. Now, please realize that I come from a United Methodist background and was taught that tongues must have interpretation. However, what I was experiencing and seeing before my eyes was the manifestation of a demon in this young man, hissing and acting like an animal, while these two other young men were speaking in a different language. It was almost as if a netting of some sort was thrown over Joe because once these two men spoke in another language this young man could not move to hurt us. So, I did the only thing I knew how. I spoke the name of Jesus Christ over and over again and commanded whatever this was to leave this young man and go back to the pit of hell where it belonged.

This lasted for about twenty seconds, but it seemed like an eternity. Then, as if nothing happened, Joe looked at me and proclaimed, "That's about what happens to me." I looked at him skeptically and asked, "Joe? Is that you?"

He said, "Yeah, it's me again."

Another important part to this story is that Joe's body language was very haughty and prideful before this happened. His eyes were almost closed shut as he looked at people, and he would hold his nose up a bit to look down to people. So, we were pretty sure this was Joe because he went back to this body language.

I made the comment, "Joe, I've never experienced these sorts of things before, but I think we might be dealing with a demon." Joe said, "You think so?" I said, "Well, when I said the name of Jes . . ."

And it started all over again – the hissing, the head cocked back, and the biting motion.

Andrew and our roadie began speaking in another language again, and this time something came to my mind. Jesus asked the man who was demon possessed what his name was, so being a man who wants to emulate Christ in all that I do, I followed His example and asked in an authoritative way, "What is your name?!"

Whatever was possessing Joe paused, looked me right in the eye and said something unintelligible. He said, "Zjetezjajehhh" or something like that.

Meanwhile Silverline's lead singer Ryan Edberg came over and said, "What are you guys doing?! We gotta get this guy in the back!"

I said, "I know but this thing keeps on manifesting itself. Whenever I say the name of Jesus Christ, it comes out."

After about ten more seconds, Joe was back with us.

So, Silverline and I took this young man to the youth

pastor's office. I went and got both youth pastors in the office. When the three of us showed up, one of the youth pastors jumped right in to deal with this demon. The other was obviously shocked and was uncertain of what to do because Joe was acting like an animal and clearly something was up. This youth pastor backed up against the wall to watch and hopefully pray.

During all of this Joe would ask us to stop for a bit for a drink of water and sometimes say, "My head hurts right here," as he pointed to an area on the right top back side of his head.

After about forty-five minutes Joe got on all fours and began panting and barking something like a dog. He was like this for about ten minutes or so.

Then the demon was gone. Joe got up and looked at us and said, "I feel so much better." His eyes were now open, and he no longer had the haughty prideful look. He was definitely different. He drank some water and thanked us, and we talked for a brief bit as his mom was coming to get him.

I learned so much on that tour about the God of the Bible. I learned a lot about myself too. I realized that what I thought God was doing in today's world was so much greater than I could have even imagined. I also realized that many of His people, including me, had put God in our "God Box" on things we didn't understand in order to feel secure and safe. But God is not some puppy. He is our Creator and not only wants to be our Lord but He wants to be our friend. The work of Christ on the cross is already finished. He has already defeated death, disease and even dying. Can the dead be raised today? I believe they can. Does God want to heal the sick, deaf, and blind? Yes! I've experienced it and I continue to experience it. He wants to work in and through us, His people! Are you willing to allow Him to work in and through you pointing people to Christ in all that you do?

God does not change. He is still very active in today's world. Are we looking and listening for where He is at work, or are we just going through life not really paying attention? Only you can really answer these questions for yourself.

*   *   *

Take time to read and pray through Acts 5:12-16:

> The apostles performed many miraculous signs and wonders among the people. And all the believers used to meet together in Solomon's Colonnade. No one else dared join them, even though they were highly regarded by the people. Nevertheless, more and more men and women believed in the Lord and were added to their number. As a result, people brought the sick into the streets and laid them on beds and mats so that at least

Peter's shadow might fall on some of them as he passed by. Crowds gathered also from the towns around Jerusalem, bringing their sick and those tormented by evil spirits, and all of them were healed.

As believers in Jesus Christ we are called to pray for people's healing. In James 5:13-16 it says the following:

Is any one of you in trouble? He should pray. Is anyone happy? Let him sing songs of praise. Is any one of you sick? He should call the elders of the church to pray over him and anoint him with oil in the name of the Lord. And the prayer offered in faith will make the sick person well; the Lord will raise him up. If he has sinned, he will be forgiven. Therefore confess your sins to each other and pray for each other so that you may be healed. The prayer of a righteous man is powerful and effective.

*   *   *

*Don't expect to build up the weak
by pulling down the strong.*
Calvin Coolidge

*   *   *

Jason DeZurik

Chapter 5

God's Way Can Be Difficult

I don't measure a man's success by how high he climbs but how high he bounces when he hits bottom.
General George S. Patton Jr.

Sometimes you think that you are not a Christian when you have trouble, but I should very much doubt whether you are a Christian at all if you did not have trouble.
Corrie ten Boom

$\mathcal{O}$ne of the ways my family and I rely not only upon God but also His people is how my family and I take care of our health care needs. If you live in the United States and are a true Christ-follower, I believe it is high time to start thinking differently and to actually practice what we see in the Bible. The biblical example in the book of Acts is clear. Acts 2:42–47 shows how the early church shared with one another and helped each other out. We can learn a lot by their example of helping one another rather than through a government program or even through health insurance. If we start living this biblical mind set, get ready for this, we may not even need health insurance. No joke!

How about cutting out the middleman and working directly with your doctor? This actually works and is in practice today by many people throughout the United States. We have been in a health cooperative called Samaritan Ministries International (www.samaritanministries.org) since 2008. There are other similar communities out there as well. We have had to deal with a broken collarbone, an asthma attack, a seizure, and even a major miscarriage, just to name a few medical needs. In this cooperative we all share in the cost of each other's health care and we pray for one another on a regular basis. My family and I have begun to eat better because we want to help others and not be a burden to the whole group. Plus, eating better has helped us realize that we needed to take responsibility for our actions, hence helping the whole cooperative. You just feel better physically, mentally, and spiritually. Yes, we feel better because of eating healthier but also because there is obviously power in prayer. We send our monthly check to other people in the cooperative that need help for that month. We write a personal check directly to them! You will notice the government and insurance companies are not involved in this process at all. It is God's people being God's people, sharing and caring for one another. Like I already said, we pray for one another and rejoice together when new children are born too. We do all of this with no health insurance or government involvement, and we deal directly with our doctors without insurance or the government denying us a claim or telling us what we can or cannot do.

I once believed that the church in Acts was promoting a way to socialism, but I couldn't have been further from the truth. Deep down I knew in my spirit that God's ways are higher than man's ways and I believe you know that in your spirit too. The government was not involved in the Acts 2 church's method of caring for each other. Yes, Christianity was illegal back then, but when anyone is forced to pay for someone else's consequences that is tyranny. There is no other word for it. I'm sure some of you might be thinking that Scripture calls us to help the poor, the orphan, and the widow. You would be correct and the early church gave us a great example of what this could look like. Christ followers are called to help the orphan, the widow, and the poor among us. We are not called to help through the government and through forced taxation. This is tyranny. So, if you are a Christ follower and believe it is good and right for the government to supply food and monetary funds to people, I would implore you to please rethink your position on this. We need to be consistent with our faith. For instance, if you don't want the government to fund abortions or any other thing you may think is immoral, then why force someone to fund something they may not want to fund? We should teach people through our actions and not force them to follow. Even Jesus didn't force people to follow Him.

Here's a question for Christians who want the federal or state government involved in our health care: Why should we involve the government? The New Testament church took responsibility in the book of Acts for themselves and shared among themselves freely without being forced.

They freely gave and shared their gifts, whether finances, food, or talents, and they freely received from everyone. I think we all could agree that something needs to change.

Instead of trying to fix a broken system, I think we should think completely outside of the box and start acting like the church of Christ that we are called to be. Let's show the world how followers of Christ really should live. Then maybe the world will start to care about receiving Jesus Christ as their Savior and live for the Lord, Jesus Christ. I don't care what you call yourself - liberal, conservative, libertarian, progressive, or whatever. If you call yourself a Christian, we need to take care of each other. How about if you're a lawyer, you share your knowledge and gifts with those in the church? Or farmers could share what they reap with the body of believers. Auto mechanics could share their talents and fix vehicles for the body. Evangelists could speak encouragement and challenging messages to the church. Engineers could use their talents and gifts for furthering the Kingdom in buildings and site work. The possibilities are endless! If everyone pitched in and did their fair share, maybe the world would finally take notice. Please consider this again as you read for yourself the early Christians' example in Acts 2:42-47:

> They devoted themselves to the apostles'
> teaching and to the fellowship, to the
> breaking of bread and to prayer. Everyone
> was filled with awe, and many wonders
> and miraculous signs were done by the
> apostles. All the believers were together and

had everything in common. Selling their
possessions and goods, they gave to anyone
as he had need. Every day they continued to
meet together in the temple courts. They
broke bread in their homes and ate together
with glad and sincere hearts, praising God
and enjoying the favor of all the people.
And the Lord added to their number daily
those who were being saved.

Remember, I am not promoting socialism or Marxism. I am
just stating what the Bible says and how we as the body of
believers are called to live. This is not just how we should
live, but what we should believe and act upon. This is
about hearing the voice of God and obeying.

As Christians, we need to take this to heart and truly not
worry about anything. We need to trust God in supplying
our needs and sustaining our lives. Jesus speaks of this in
Matthew 6:25-34:

Therefore I tell you, do not worry about
your life, what you will eat or drink; or
about your body, what you will wear. Is not
life more than food, and the body more than
clothes? Look at the birds of the air; they do
not sow or reap or store away in barns, and
yet your heavenly Father feeds them. Are
you not much more valuable than they?
Can any one of you by worrying add a
single hour to your life?

And why do you worry about clothes? See how the flowers of the field grow. They do not labor or spin. Yet I tell you that not even Solomon in all his splendor was dressed like one of these. If that is how God clothes the grass of the field, which is here today and tomorrow is thrown into the fire, will he not much more clothe you — you of little faith? So do not worry, saying, 'What shall we eat?' or 'What shall we drink?' or 'What shall we wear?' For the pagans run after all these things, and your heavenly Father knows that you need them. But seek first his kingdom and his righteousness, and all these things will be given to you as well. Therefore do not worry about tomorrow, for tomorrow will worry about itself. Each day has enough trouble of its own.

So do you actually believe this? Are you living this out today?

How much more valuable are you and your family than the flowers of the field or the birds of the air? You are much more valuable because you are created in the image of God. Do not have a worldly mindset and run after trivial things. Trust your heavenly Father. He will supply no matter what you are going through. It may not look like how you want it to look, but He will answer you.

Are you willing to allow the Holy Spirit to live in and

through you?

My family and I are doing our best to actually put this teaching into practice in all that we do. We have been learning to trust other Christ-followers to hear God's voice and obey as well. Sometimes, as you have already read about, God puts it on people's hearts to help us out in some way. Hopefully, you have already begun to realize that the Christ-follower must not only hear God's voice and know what to do but he or she must obey. We cannot just hear God's leading and then do nothing. We must do what He is calling us to do. What is so amazing is when He calls us as a family to do something that just makes no sense at all. There are times we have been asked to help someone in a financial way when we think we cannot afford it, or to help someone with our time when we think we don't even have enough time for ourselves. But God blesses us right back. In fact, in the past we have actually sent money to someone we were led to help and soon afterward we received what we gave to the ministry or people -- and sometimes it's even more than we were led to give. It is not unusual for us to receive an envelope in the mail with cash in it from an anonymous person. God has supplied our needs in this way many times before.

Keep in mind that everything belongs to the God of the Bible. If He really is the Creator of the universe, then He owns it all. I write this because sometimes we do not receive financially in return, and I will be very blunt, this can be very difficult. We are blessed by giving and we keep James 1:12 in mind: "Blessed is the man who perseveres under trial, because when he has stood the test, he will receive the crown of life that God has promised to those who love Him." There are times that the Lord may want you to learn something under a trying time.

Being consistent with Scripture is important. Remember that Jesus said this in John 8:31-32: "If you hold to my teaching, you are really my disciples. Then you will know the truth, and the truth will set you free." Hold to His teachings, and the truth will set you free. Seek Him out. You will not be sorry! Your adventure in serving the God of the universe is ready to begin. All you need to do is say yes to this adventure of being in a right relationship with the King of the Universe, Jesus Christ. I cannot promise you an easy life at all but I can promise you that God's plan for the life he has given to you is the best plan available to you.

Through my travels around the country, I am blessed to meet so many wonderful, caring people who are not afraid to serve God. I also meet many people who call themselves Christians; yet I can't help but wonder if they are really following Christ. Many people claim to be Christ-followers, but when their lives are examined there is not much proof to be found in their actions that they are actually followers of Christ. There should be biblical actions to go along with our words. What I mean is in our everyday life actions we should exemplify what the Bible promotes as living for God.

I write this not to judge but to get us to think about and examine ourselves. I believe Jesus when He said in

Matthew 7:13-14:

> Enter through the narrow gate. For wide is
> the gate and broad is the road that leads to
> destruction, and many enter through it. But
> small is the gate and narrow the road that
> leads to life, and only a few find it. ✳

We have been designed by God to follow Him. He placed
within us a desire to worship Him. However, Satan takes
what God means for good and twists it. For instance, Satan
used Scripture to tempt Jesus to sin. However, Jesus
quoted Scripture to combat Satan and cut through his lies.
You can find this in Matthew 4. Friends, when you commit
Scripture to memory in your mind and heart, it is one of
the best ways to be on the attack against Satan's wiles.

Satan can make sin look so appealing sometimes. From the
earliest days of the world, Satan has twisted the truth to
try to draw mankind away from God. He convinced Adam
and Eve in the Garden that the forbidden fruit was
appealing and harmless. They succumbed to his conniving
ways and chose to disobey God, introducing sin and death
into the world.

God told Adam from which tree he should avoid eating
fruit and informed him of the consequences he would
receive if he sinned against God. He gave Adam and Eve
free will.

Did you spot the morsel of wisdom there?

In that little story, God showed us an incredible lesson in

being a godly parent. He showed us that we should not force our children to obey. As Ephesians 6:4 instructs, we should not exasperate our children.

I can imagine that those of you who are younger reading this right now are thinking, "Sweet! See, we can do anything we want." Well, yes, that is true, but there is a catch: each one of us must face the consequences of our actions.

As parents, we need to teach our children that there are consequences to our actions, just as God taught Adam and Eve. In fact, the human race is still reaping incredible strife from the choice they made to disobey God. But don't blame them; we would have done the same thing.

I know that consequences of bad decisions can hurt and are painful for a time, but punishment for wrong actions is not meant to be enjoyable. It should be used to teach us what we should and should not do. By accepting the consequences of our actions, we learn personal responsibility and how to be a person who is disciplined in our lives. We learn to mature and stop being children. I understand that as a young person you want to feel and be treated like an adult. I know I did, especially in my teen years. Keep in mind, however, that it can be a painful but rewarding path to learn to be a responsible adult and to live a godly life that is pleasing to our Lord.

Here are my challenges to you:

1) **Start to become observant of Satan's temptations when he twists the truth to try to draw you away from obeying**

God.

A wise man told me once, "Character is not built in trials. Character is built before the trials begin." Such wisdom.

One way this happens is by reading God's Word and being open to what the Holy Spirit is trying to teach you. I also encourage you to find a man or woman of God who can help train you up in God's ways. I am not talking about a pastor here. I am encouraging you to find someone that you know is a follower of Christ through their example of living their life for God. Slow down and pray.

✳ 2) **Begin memorizing Scripture and storing it away in your heart.**

When Satan does tempt you and twists the Word of God, you will be ready to attack with the truth of God's Word like Jesus did. However, when you do give in to Satan's bidding, as we all do at times, stand up and accept the consequences of your decision. Not only will you be less inclined to make the same mistake again, but you will also be taking a step toward a godly life of obedience as a spiritually mature adult. This is something all of us need to work on every single day with the help of the Holy Spirit.

Don't know where to start memorizing? Here are some suggestions: ✳

Psalm 1 - James 1 - Hebrews 5:11–6:6
1 Peter 4:1–19 - Ephesians 6:1–4 - Proverbs 22

3) Do a self-examination to see if you are really trusting in God or not.

Read these words of Jesus in Matthew 6:25-34 (below) very carefully. Are you actually doing this and being consistent with the Scripture, or are you worrying? Are you actually trusting your heavenly Father?

> Therefore I tell you, do not worry about your life, what you will eat or drink; or about your body, what you will wear. Is not life more important than food, and the body more important than clothes? Look at the birds of the air; they do not sow or reap or store away in barns, and yet your heavenly Father feeds them. Are you not much more valuable than they? Who of you by worrying can add a single hour to his life?

> And why do you worry about clothes? See how the lilies of the field grow. They do not labor or spin. Yet I tell you that not even Solomon in all his splendor was dressed like one of these. If that is how God clothes the grass of the field, which is here today and tomorrow is thrown into the fire, will he not much more clothe you, O you of little faith? So do not worry, saying, 'What shall we eat?' or 'What shall we drink?' or 'What shall we wear?' For the pagans run after all these things, and your heavenly Father knows that you need them. But seek first his

kingdom and his righteousness, and all these things will be given to you as well. Therefore do not worry about tomorrow, for tomorrow will worry about itself. Each day has enough trouble of its own.

Ask the Lord for help in following this Scripture. Start living this out everyday. Instead of worrying, tell God, "I'm trusting in you today."

Keep a good attitude and realize that everything may not work out as you planned it but that it's okay.

*   *   *

If God really does own it all then trust Him already.

Dear Lord,

I'm trusting in You today + everyday. I know I may fail but when I do I promise to go back to these Scripture + remember You take care of my every need. I'm more valuable than the birds because I was made in Your image. Thank you Lord, for Your word, for always taking care of my every need + for creating me to be like You. In Jesus. Name Amen

Jason DeZurik

Chapter 6

Free Will

Man will ultimately be governed by God or by tyrants.
Benjamin Franklin

Being a role model is the most powerful form of educating...too often fathers neglect it because they get so caught up in making a living they forget to make a life.
John Wooden

$\mathcal{I}$ really like having my morning cup of coffee. When I make my morning coffee it usually isn't such a chore, but one morning I learned a very valuable lesson.

I put the coffee in the filter, poured the appropriate amount of water into the coffee maker, and then went to read my Bible. After about ten minutes I went to go get a freshly brewed cup of coffee. To my surprise and annoyance, my freshly made pot of coffee was all over the counter, and had even found its way under the microwave. Oh joy! The pot was only a quarter full and there was still water in the coffee maker trying to push its way into the pot through the plugged filter area.

I was not pleased.

I questioned, "Why did this happen? God, you know I've got a lot to do today!"

I kept my composure though and proceeded to clean up the mess. After what seemed like an eternity of cleaning, I came to realize who the culprit was of this little inconvenience. It was me! Big shock, right?

No one else had touched this coffee maker but I was to the point of getting rid of the coffee maker thinking there must be something wrong with it. It must be on its last leg. The reality of the matter was that even though I wasn't in the room, in my haste, I had created this mess. I had accidently poured coffee grounds not only into the coffee filter but also into where the coffee filter goes. I had unknowingly plugged it myself.

The Lord showed me two things through this little bit of excitement.

❋ **First**: Keep a good attitude. Philippians 4:4 says, "Rejoice in the Lord always. I will say it again: Rejoice!"

❋ **Second, and I think even more important**: When things aren't going your way and you don't know what caused an issue in your life, relax and look at yourself first.

Instead of trying to point fingers at someone (or in this case something) else, look at yourself and see what you might have done to cause this problem or conflict. The reality is that you can only work on you.

We all seem to want to help or fix others; the truth of the matter is we need to take more responsibility for our own actions. We need to look and see how God wants to use us for His kingdom and be willing to grow spiritually, mentally, and physically. When we allow the Holy Spirit to work on us is when we will see the world change for Christ.

It has taken me quite a while to grasp the following concept but I think I have finally taken hold of it: The God who created us and put us on this planet loves us so much that He desires us to love Him freely. However, in order for this to happen, He must be willing to allow us to go against Him and His ways.

For instance, He has given us rules and guidelines by which we are to live in this world. Ten of them are found in Exodus 20. They are called the ten commandments. One of these tells us to worship no other gods but Him. So if we worship only this God who created the whole universe out of nothing, He will be pleased and we would not be sinning in that. But will God allow us to choose to worship another god or ourselves in place of the one true God? Yes. He loves us so much that He will allow us to turn our backs on Him. Does He want it to happen? Of course not. But He is willing to allow it to happen. Will God allow us to choose to have sex with someone other than our husband or wife? The answer is yes. Will God allow us to choose to disobey and dishonor our parents? Again the answer is yes. He loves us so much that He allows His creation to go against Him. He does not force us to love Him or to do His will. He doesn't force us to obey.

This is where His people come in. Christ's followers are called to speak the truth in love. I believe this means that we must tell – sometimes warn – people what the truth is. If these people choose to follow Him, that is between them and God. Should they choose not to follow God and His ways, that again is between them and God. Even if they do not believe in Him, it is their free will to choose. Are you willing to love as much as God does or at least strive to do that? We are called to love. In other words, we need to tell people the truth and leave it up to them to believe or not. If they choose not to believe, the Lord will deal with them, be it ever so severely.

This also goes for our own Christian brothers and sisters. You can tell people the truth about helping the poor and poverty stricken; however, once you force people to help them, you have stepped over the line.

A great example of this is the account of Ananias and Sapphira in Acts 5. They sold a piece of property and said they gave all of the money from the sale to the church. A quick check on the context of this passage shows us that the early believers in Christ began to sell their possessions and goods for the betterment of the whole body of Christ (the church). You will notice that they were not forced to do this and were not required to give everything to the group, for Peter says in Acts 5:3-4:

Ananias, how is it that Satan has so filled
your heart that you have lied to the Holy
Spirit and have kept for yourself some of
the money you received for the land? Didn't
it belong to you before it was sold? And
after it was sold wasn't the money at your
disposal? What made you think of doing
such a thing? You have not lied to men but
to God.

Ananias and his wife Sapphira owned a field and sold it.
They told the church that they gave them all of the money
from the sale when they had actually kept part of the sale
for themselves. So their sin wasn't that they kept part of
the money. In fact, Peter never mentions that! What did he
mention? He points out their sin was lying to the Holy
Spirit.

I think it is also easy to deduce that part of their sin was
their desire to receive praise and glory that they did not
deserve. If they had given all of their money, I think they
would have received a blessing. If they had given only part
of the money and had been honest and actually told the
truth, I think they still would have been fine. The point is
that God is the judge, not humans. Their consequence for
lying was instant death. This helps us to see that the
choices we make have consequences – good and bad. We
can either choose to live God's way or not.

People's choices affect more than just themselves; they
affect others as well, sometimes for the good and
sometimes for the bad. Here's the hard part, if you are a

follower of Christ and want to live His way I encourage you to be like our Creator. He didn't force Adam and Eve to follow Him. He gave them a choice to go against Him. Even Jesus Christ in Matthew 19:16-22 gave the rich young ruler the option to follow Him or not. Forcing people to follow God's ways is not freedom at all.

Let me try to further illustrate this point that people need the liberty to make their own choices while we do not force people to follow God's good and right ways. As of this edition of this book, my wife and I have a daughter who is five years old. We love her very much. She has her own will to do what she likes and will do what she pleases. By the time she was two years old we had trained her that she needed to obey the first time. Does she always obey the first time? No. As her father, though, I would be doing a terrible job raising her if I did not correct her actions now that are sinful. For instance, if I didn't expect and require first time obedience from her, what would I be teaching her even at this young age? I would be teaching her that she does not need to obey the first time I tell her to do something. If I tell her to stop running somewhere, and after the third or fourth time she finally obeys, that could be a serious problem or at least the potential to be one. Even as young as eight months old we had already started training her about the importance of obeying the first time. As early as twelve months she may have run out into the street and got injured if she was not taught to obey us the first time. It is a parent's job to train a child to do this. Unfortunately, many children are taught at a young age to only obey after the third or fourth time. And if children aren't corrected at this young age, many of us know the teen years would be quite a challenge.

This is why being a parent is such a huge responsibility. We are to train our children to know why it's important to accept Jesus as Savior. We are also to teach them to follow Jesus Christ and hear and obey the Holy Spirit. They still make their own choice but as parents we need to be willing to lead not only by our words but our actions as well. For teenagers and even young adults reading this, remember you need to honor and obey your parents. It is commanded of you. Once you move out of the house then you are truly free to do your will but be ready for the consequences of your sinful actions or the blessings you'll receive for following Christ. It's your choice though. Don't forget too that all of us need to honor our parents because for our whole lives we are never entirely removed from that command.

I want to challenge you to not just be saved in the name of Jesus Christ, but also to be hearers and doers of the Word of God. We need to obey God's leading. You need to obey God's leading. Hear the Holy Spirit and obey. If you've messed up, our heavenly Father is there to welcome you back into His loving arms. He loves you so much!

*   *   *

For further study on this, read Luke 15:11-32 and James 2:1-26.

Jason DeZurik

Chapter 7

Lead By Example

Always do everything you ask of those you command.
General George S. Patton Jr.

Leadership means setting the example.
Lee Iacocca

In my first year as a youth minister, I took a group of students and adults to Toronto, Canada for a mission trip.

The mission organization's group leaders took us to a park that, in the evening, was known for immoral activity but during the day was safe (at least that's what they told us). So we took our group of high school students and adult leaders to this park and began to worship God through music and interacting with the few people that we could see in the park. As we began to play music, something very interesting happened: people we hadn't seen in the bushes and surrounding areas came out to join us. It was obvious that many of these people were homeless or didn't have anything except for the clothes on their backs. Some of them began to worship with us and others just needed someone to listen as they talked.

While we continued to worship, I noticed a man coming toward us who looked as if he had been in a fight not long before our arrival in the park. As he came closer, I realized that this man was covered in blood. I assumed it was from some altercation the night before. To this day I do not know if it was his own blood or someone else's, but I will tell you what went through my mind:

- I immediately thought of the safety of these students and adults for which I was responsible.

- Since I didn't know what he needed or if he was dangerous, I immediately began to consider how I could keep this man a safe distance from everyone.

- I thought of my wife whom I had married ten months earlier, our relationship, and our first child with whom she was pregnant.

- I was very afraid as I thought of my new family, for I didn't know if I would contract some sort of disease from this blood-covered man.

I walked toward him as he approached to keep him a safe distance from everyone else, and then it happened! As the man approached me, he stuck out his hand to shake mine in friendship. I was frozen for what seemed like a minute, but I'm sure it was only about a second. What should I do? Then my spirit heard the voice of God say, "Jesus would touch this man." I knew I had only a split second to obey or disobey God's leading. I could either touch this man and quite possibly ruin my life, getting injured or stabbed myself, or I could keep him away from me and everyone else so that we were safe, getting him help later. The big question was should I touch him as Jesus would have touched a leper and welcome him into the group?

I am pleased to say that God gave me the strength to obey His leading. I stuck out my hand. We shook hands and then embraced. We talked for a while, and our group not only got him something to eat, but also got him to the right people for help.

I tell you this story so you understand the importance of your actions and obeying God's voice when He asks you to do something for Him. You see, your life is not your own. It belongs to God.

I can also tell you, I believe, that this one event in a large park in Canada changed the entire scope of the youth ministry at the church I was serving and in the surrounding community when we returned home.

Why?

Because I heard and obeyed God's voice, those students as well as the adult leaders knew that I was completely sold out to Christ. They knew that I was willing to put my life on the line to not only help others for the Lord but also to further Christ's Kingdom.

I am pleased to say that this one event continued the

revolution Jesus Christ started over 2,000 years ago, in many people in our community through the youth ministry in that congregation. That ministry continues to grow to this day throughout the world. Many of these students are now adults that not only are in ministry positions but understand the importance of living their lives for Christ in all aspects of life.

All I did was follow Jesus' example in ministry! We all need to do the same right now. We need not fear humans or the circumstances we are in; we must only fear and respect God. Only when we grasp and live by this concept will we start to see some progress in society. Jesus trained His disciples by being with them and showing them how to live. He sunk His life into them. If you are a youth leader, pastor, or other Christian leader in your community, who are your disciples? Are they learning how to live the way of Christ or the way of humans? If you are a Christ-follower, whether you are in a leadership position or not, who are your disciples or who are you discipling? Just because you are a blue-collar worker or a white collar worker or a stay at home mom or a busy father doesn't let you off the hook. We are all called to make disciples of Jesus Christ! Yes, even the young person reading this right now.

Be honest with yourself because the goal is to find truth. So don't cheat yourself and say something like, "Oh, I'm fine the way I am. I don't need to disciple anyone and no one needs to disciple me."

To that I say, "Oh really?" Even Jesus had disciples, and he commanded us to go into all the world and make disciples! I hope the following story inspires you to not only be wise in how you act toward non-believers and those who are more immature spiritually than you but more importantly how you need to live out the teachings of God's Word in every area of your life. If Christ-followers would actually do this instead of just saying we are, I believe it will change the world.

Early on in my youth ministry experience, the adult leaders and I had opportunities to impact many students from broken homes. One student in particular had just moved into our community with his mom and stepfather while his biological father lived about an hour away.

This student not only had a strange last name that other students would make fun of, but he was a little overweight too. So, not only was he the new kid but his parents had just divorced, he had a funny last name, and he was rounder than most students. What a way to start out huh?

Well, he started coming to our youth ministry. To be honest, he seemed to have trouble at first fitting in. He could play a really mean game of ping pong though, so that helped him gain some respect in our group. I took a liking to this kid almost immediately. Why? He was a student who needed some loving and guidance really bad, and he was available. He was always around. Not at first but, I think it is safe to say he and I grew a tight bond together. I loved him. Heck, I still love him! He's a great kid, even though he is a grown man now.

Anyway, you get the idea. We began to hang out a lot. We found out that we had a lot in common. He loved music. I love music. He loved video games. I loved video games. Even though he wouldn't have known the word to say, he wanted me to disciple him. I wanted to disciple him. We spent many a night after youth group just sitting in my car or his car in his driveway just talking and speaking life into one another. I've had the blessing of discipling many students over the years who I would have loved to have as my own children. He was one of these students.

I believe the Bible and teach the creation account in the Bible to be true. Obviously, I speak on other things too, but this is just one of them. So, after about one year of discipling him, we were again just sitting in his driveway talking and he dropped a big question on me.

He said, "My dad (his biological father who lived an hour away) tells me that evolution is true and that you are wrong about creation being only six days long. He thinks you're crazy. What should I do, because I don't believe him? I believe you and think he is wrong. I want to tell him that you are right and he is wrong."

WHOA! I realized in that moment I had a huge decision to make. I could:

- Tell him how wrong his dad was and defend my position on creation, badmouthing his father in the process.
- Tell him that his dad was probably right and I'm just messed up.
- Tell him to honor his father.

I chose to encourage him to honor and to obey his father. Why? I chose that because that was his dad; and if I truly believed the Bible, then God had given that son to that father for a reason. I needed to honor God's decision. I told this young man, "Even though I disagree with your father, he is your dad and you must give him respect."

This young man said, "Yeah, but you're right about creation."

I told him, "That may be true, but that is your dad. You must honor and respect him, even if that means you cannot be a part of this youth group anymore. You must obey him. Your father will be here long after I am gone. He's your blood. I am only in your life for a short season. In time he will come to know the truth. Stay strong and honor him no matter what."

Well, he must have listened to what I had said because two years later his biological father showed up to a church event where we had a creation scientist speaking. I was already nervous about having this event in our town, but knowing this father was in the audience heightened my anxiety.

After the event this father approached me. We had never met until this very moment. Saying I was nervous would be an understatement. Would he be angry or just confrontational?

He stuck out his hand to shake mine and I grabbed it. He said, "My name is [so and so]. For some reason my son thinks you are pretty cool. Regarding this creation subject, I definitely don't agree with you; but you can hang out with my son any time you want. Thanks for loving my son."

I was speechless. I was so shocked because it never even crossed my mind that he might say something like that. Just thinking about it brings tears to my eyes. I finally said, "Thanks. You really have a great son." He said, "Thanks." And that was the end of it.

We must remember as Christ-followers that we are not here to win arguments. We are here to hear God's voice and obey. Sometimes that does mean we stand our ground and make a point, but other times it means we keep our mouths shut. We do all of this in love.

I once had an amazing discipler who put it this way: "If we don't do everything in love and remember that we need to love, it is all worthless. Anything we do won't matter at all." I believe he is completely right. He believed this so much that he wouldn't even begin to disciple me until I had all of I Corinthians 13 memorized. That is how much he believed what he was saying. I have, personally, found that to be true.

If we get the love part wrong, what's the point?

*   *   *

After reading these stories from my life, this is my challenge to you.

Write down at least three people you need to spend time with and disciple. If you are already meeting with these people, then I encourage you to ask God if you should start spending even more time with them. ① Isabel

Who is discipling you? If you have no one then you need to find someone. Be careful with whom you choose.

First, seek God's leading in this. Listen, speak and listen some more. ✻

Secondly, make sure that this person is a person of godly character and integrity. If they are not, run the other way and find someone else. This is very important.

Dear Lord,
Please bring a godly person who has integrity in my life. I need someone to disciple me. Help me to listen + seek Your leading. Help me to disciple Izzy. Help me to always love in everything I do + say. In Jesus Name, Amen

Jason DeZurik

Chapter 8

How Did It Come To This?

*A thorough knowledge of the Bible
is worth more than a college education.*
Theodore Roosevelt

*In the beginning was Jesus and Jesus was with God
and Jesus was God. Jesus was with God in the beginning.
Through Jesus all things were made
without Jesus nothing was made that has been made.*
Apostle John / John 1:1-3 (paraphrase)

When I was around the age of four, my mother started taking my sister and me to church in small town America. North Branch, Minnesota to be exact. A couple years later, my dad had a horrific automobile accident, in which he could have easily perished. After that accident he became a believer in Jesus Christ and our whole family started attending church almost every Sunday and later on almost every Wednesday night up until I graduated from high school.

I learned about all the Bible stories and learned good godly ways and even went to a Christian school for four years. Once I left the Christian school for public school in seventh grade, something changed. In our science class we started to be taught about the theory of evolution as well as the big bang theory. I would ask questions to myself but never really engage the teacher because, well, he was my teacher. At the time, in my mind, he knew better. So, I just listened and didn't really question too much. As time went on I began to logically see that if this theory of evolution and the big bang theory were true, then some things in the Bible couldn't be true. It was a serious crisis that I had on my hands.

I really didn't start asking questions of people until my eighth grade year because I processed this for about a year in my mind. For instance, I would ask myself the following questions during this self-examination:

- If evolution is true and we descended from creatures like monkeys, fish, and even smaller creatures, then how did this happen and how can it fit with the Bible and its explanation for life?

- If evolution is true and death is the mechanism for this theory to work, then how can the Bible be true? According to the Bible, death, disease, and dying did not enter the universe until after Adam sinned against God. According to the Bible, the creation God made was very good. Death is not very good.

- If evolution is true, then what makes us different from the animals or are we no different from them?

These are just some of the questions I asked myself over this very important time of my life. To those of you wondering if a child at that age can ask themselves questions like this, the answer is an absolute yes.

So in eighth grade I went to my pastor at the time and asked him one very pointed question. Our conversation went something like this:

Me: Pastor, I have been learning about the theory of evolution in school and I have been really thinking about this. It seems to contradict what the Bible has to say and what it teaches about the origins of the universe. The Bible teaches the story about Adam and Eve and that God created in six days. Evolution teaches that over a long period of time, everything evolved and that humans eventually evolved from monkeys (I should have said, "something like monkeys"). Which theory is true?

Pastor: Oh, I know this is hard to understand and it is hard to explain but we are learning more and more every day about how things work. Scientists are starting to show us new things and how they really work. The creation story probably isn't exactly accurate, but what counts is the truth found in the story of the Biblical creation story. All we need to know is that we need a Savior to save us from our sins so what really counts in all of it is Jesus.

And with that, I began the slow downward spiral of completely losing my faith not only in God and the Bible, but in people as well. My whole life I had been told these stories in the Bible were true and could be trusted. After all, I was taught the Bible is the Word of God. It could be trusted. Now I had a pastor, the guy who was supposed to believe this stuff, tell me it was not true. He and many pastors today do not understand the great damage they inflict on students at a very young age when they do not stay consistent with the teaching of God's Word. (Pastors and church leaders: I know many of you want to be loving and direct these students down the right path but you also MUST give them the truth. Truth and love must go hand in hand. They should not be separated.)

So I moved to other questions after this:

- If that part wasn't true, then what else wasn't true?

  o Did the flood of Noah's time happen?

  o Did a fish really swallow up a guy for three days and the guy lived?

  o Did a bunch of people really march around a city, and the walls fell down?

  o Did fire from heaven actually come down for Elijah's sacrifice?

As I grew up, these questions even moved to the one that this pastor said was so important about Jesus mattering. If Jesus Christ really matters then why does He matter? Why?

You must answer this question.

According to Scripture, Jesus came to be our Lord and Savior. But, our Savior from WHAT?! Stop and think about this for a bit. What is Jesus saving us from?

This is a very easy answer IF you believe the Genesis account of creation. If you do not believe it, you will have a tough time and you will have to do some major mental gymnastics.

Jesus came to save us from . . . drum roll please . . . DEATH!

Before sin entered into creation, there was no death. If death were here from the beginning of time (as the theory of evolution promotes), then according to the Biblical account we see in Genesis 1, death would not only be good, but it would be very good. Right?

> God saw all that he had made, and it was
> very good. And there was evening, and
> there was morning — the sixth day. Genesis
> 1:31

I'm not at all trying to be difficult. I'm just asking us all to be consistent. Obviously, death is not good, let alone very good! If it were, we would be happy and excited when someone died. Generally, though, this is a sad time even when many of us try to make a funeral about celebrating life today. Death is still sad. Dying is sad and so is disease. If it isn't sad or a result of our sin, then why do we try to stop cancer from happening with all of the research and fundraising events? If Alzheimer's and dementia are so wonderful, why are we looking for ways to defeat it? I know some of you think that maybe it is good. Why do I know this? I know this because I run into people all the time who try to justify man's view of the world and turn a straightforward reading of scripture on its head. In Romans 6:23 it says, "For the wages of sin is death but the gift of God is eternal life through Christ Jesus our Lord." Scripture is clear that our sin against God is the reason that death is here.

As human beings most of us are trying to stop the consequence of the curse all the time. Here are two examples below to help make my point:

- We raise and spend a lot of money to try to not only stop cancer, but also to find a cure for this horrific disease.

- We spend oodles of money to help keep people alive even when it seems there is no hope.

As Christians, when we compromise on not only such a basic tenant of the faith, but one that is so central to the Good News message of Jesus Christ, we confuse not only believers, but also non-believers who are genuinely searching for the truth. I wish we wouldn't make this so hard, but I do believe I know why we do it. We are afraid of what other people will think or say about us. We are afraid we might look foolish in man's eyes. Why? Well, let me ask you some questions and tell you a story.

If God Himself told everyone that He created everything in six earth days while our time was moving, would you believe Him? I am asking this of people who follow Christ and His teachings. Said another way, if the Creator of the universe informed us inside of our time, while our time was moving, that He created the universe in six literal days as we know them, would you believe Him?

These are questions I wrestled with on a daily basis since being in junior high. I began to ask the following:

- Can the Bible be trusted?

- Is the God of the Bible good?

- If God is so good and powerful, why is there death in the world?

- Is the God of the Bible perfect?

- Can the God of the Bible lie?

- What does the word "holy" mean?

- Is the God of the Bible holy?

- Is God inside or outside of time? Or both?

I dug even deeper and I asked these questions to people who were believers in Jesus and many would give favorable answers. Many were not pastors. I would ask them, "Can God be trusted?" They would answer with an unequivocal, "yes." Then I would ask, "So you believe God created in six days?" Many times they would answer, "Well no, but what matters is Jesus." Or I would ask, "Can the God of the Bible lie?" And I would usually get a very strong answer of, "No." Then I would ask about the creation days or about the miracles like Jonah in the big fish or about the parting of the Red Sea. Many times, but not always, they would say something like, "Well, we don't know if that is true, but what really matters is Jesus." As you can see, I got virtually the same answer from these believers in Jesus Christ as from my pastor.

So I researched Jesus. Who was He and why did He come? In simple terms, I came to realize that He came to defeat the curse placed on us through sin. What is the curse? Death. So, I saw the inconsistency of people and realized that if Genesis is not true, then the entire Bible has some serious issues. As I grew up, I started realizing that many people who claimed to follow Jesus didn't seem to believe this part of the Bible. This led me to just keep going down a path of secularism and I eventually became a devout believer in the theory of evolution, thinking it was entirely factual. I not only gave up my faith in Jesus Christ, but I also completely denied the existence of any supreme being. For all intents and purposes, I became an atheist. I logically came to the conclusion that if evolution were true, we are all just accidents with no purpose and I might as well party it up and have fun. I decided to enjoy the time I have here because it's all the time I have. No God means no afterlife or anything after death, so there's no heaven or hell. That was very freeing, or so I thought.

My senior year of high school I really began to live for myself. If evolution was true, I logically came to the conclusion that no one makes the rules, and all current rules of society are just made up and can be changed. So, if no one can really know the truth and how things work, this means that the rules can change with no consequences. The truth of the matter was that I willingly began to run toward a sinful lifestyle, but it didn't matter anymore to me because no one was really in charge. I deduced, and I believe rightfully so, that if the theory of evolution were true, then I would live out the survival of the fittest to its utmost and beat down any competition. After all, if we are basically just animals, we should act as such.

Making this decision almost ruined my life. I moved to Seattle to pursue my dream of becoming a rock star and pursued that dream for six years. Thank the Lord, He never gave up on me even though I was selfish and hurt many people along the way. Some were really good friends and really trusted me, but to my shame, I was only in it for myself.

I was, at least in my mind, starting to become "someone" and moving forward in life. However, I was unhappy and depressed quite a bit. I don't think anyone (other than my family) ever really knew the struggle I had going on inside of me because I was a pretty happy-go-lucky guy with a good number of friends, acquaintances, and associates. I found happiness in things of this world like alcohol, women, partying, and money.

God knew what I needed, though, and He put an amazing person into my life just as I was about to go over the edge. To this day, this person has no idea how much he helped me out. I cannot find him. Even with Internet searches and such I don't know where he is. His name is Danny Castro and I would love to find him and talk to him again some day.

Danny and I would have very deep conversations about the meaning of life, evolution, and God. We would get into discussions and I would tell him how crazy he was because evolution, at least in my mind, had proven much of the Bible to be wrong; you couldn't believe an old book that was put together by who knows whom. He would come right back with something like the following statement: "That's very interesting; how do you know that to be true?" Round and round we would go. What was so good about this relationship was he allowed me to seek and search out answers for myself. I could swear, yell, or whatever; he loved and accepted me for who I was. Sometimes he'd point me in a direction but he never once (not that I can remember anyway) said, "You're wrong." He would just say, "That's very interesting; why do you believe that?" Or he would say, "Can you show me where you got that information?" He really challenged me to think through what I believed to be true. He really stretched my thinking and lovingly showed me the truth.

Now, I want to be clear about something. I was completely open to let the truth lead me to wherever it would lead. I was not afraid to be wrong. If I were right, then I would defend my position very passionately.

Danny started helping me to see that much of what I thought was true or factual really wasn't factual at all. He helped me to see that scientists are just people who have a bias just like we all have.

Please do not take offense to the following statement: Scientists are not as objective as we have been led to believe.

I am not saying scientists are bad people. I love science! What I believe is all scientists come with a bias whether they are biased for creation or biased toward evolution. It means we need to take what they have to say with a grain of salt and test it like anything else. If it passes the scientific method, then there might be something to it. If what they are saying or promoting has been based on a test or research that we know to be faulty, then we can probably dismiss it. I have come to realize that things we think are true regarding the universe and our planet that scientists say are facts, aren't always facts. We need to make sure we investigate HOW they came to their conclusions. This must also be done with Scripture as well and people's interpretations of it. I have come to the conclusion that if you truly seek out truth you will find it. The question you must be willing to answer is whether or not you are willing to be open to the truth even if it goes against what you've been taught to be truth in the past. This includes us all.

As I was being challenged in my beliefs out in Seattle I became even more restless realizing that what I had come to believe had some serious holes in it. I would read books and talk to many people about this subject of origins and the way things worked. I got so restless that I would walk the streets of Seattle at night sometimes yelling at the top of my lungs asking God if He were real. I did this for about four months.

Searching. Seeking. Finding Truth!

Question: Are you willing to head where truth leads no matter what?

Please think about this and pray about your answer.

Please give an honest answer. You will only be cheating yourself if you lie on this one.

Jesus said in John 14:6–7, "I am the way and the truth and the life. No one comes to the Father except through me. If you really knew me, you would know my Father as well. From now on, you do know him and have seen him."

✳ Out of Jesus' own mouth we know He is the way to heaven (not a way), He is the truth (not a truth), and He is the life (not a life). He has made it clear that the way to the Father is through Him and the way to eternal life is through Him. Wherever truth is, it is from Him because Jesus Christ is truth. ✳

As Christians, we must base our lives off of Scripture,

When we find something that is not in the Bible we need to measure it and check it against Scripture. When we hear teaching that sounds good and we know truth is in it but something just doesn't seem right, we need to search and seek for truth.

What do I mean? I think we can agree that stealing and murder are wrong. They are truths found in the ten commandments given to us by God Himself. Did you know that He wrote those with His very own finger? Deuteronomy 9:10 tells us this:

> The LORD gave me two stone tablets
> inscribed by the finger of God. On them
> were all the commandments the LORD
> proclaimed to you on the mountain out of
> the fire, on the day of the assembly.

Pretty cool huh? The ten commandments are directly from God Himself. Moses did not etch them out, God did with His finger. More on this later in chapter nine.

Anyway, we know these truths: do not steal and do not murder. Let's say we find a teaching that agrees with these truths. This teaching we can all agree is true. But what if the person teaching the truth then says, "Now that we know stealing and murdering are wrong, let us praise our leader and wise man, Buddha."

We measure this teaching against Scripture found in the Bible because all of the Bible is based on truth. The Bible is very clear that we should not follow other gods and we are to not worship any graven image. So, a teaching that says to worship Buddha is false. How do we know this? We measure everything by God's Word, the Bible.

It really is quite easy to employ this technique, but here's the kicker. You must be in the Word of God in order not to be held captive by hollow and deceptive philosophies as it states in Colossians 2:8, "See to it that no one takes you captive through hollow and deceptive philosophy, which depends on human tradition and the basic principles of this world rather than on Christ."

If you are a Christ-follower, you need to figure out what the Bible teaches about the questions in Appendix 1, and then you need to base your life off of the truth you learn. Take time to pray and ask God for guidance as you write down your answers in Appendix 1. I have given you some Scriptures to look up to help you get started.

I will give you my answers to these questions in the next chapter for what I believe I have found to be true, but I encourage you to seek it out for yourself.

If we are to be consistent with Scripture, we need to believe Scripture from the very first verse.

*　　*　　*

For further study I encourage you to read John 1:1–18. It really does come down to Jesus.

Who is he? *He is the Christ. The Son of the Living God.*

Then take time to read Genesis chapters 1 – 3 taking time to see that Jesus Christ was there at the beginning.

Lastly, read two great resources:
Evolution: The Lie, **written by Ken Ham**
Mere Christianity, **Written by C.S.Lewis**

- Jesus is the true Light.
- The Word was God.

firmament : The heavens or the sky.
hollow : empty, void, unfilled.
  without significance. meaningless. worthless.
    valueless. fruitless.
Deceptive: misleading - Tricky, untrustworthy.
Philosophy: human teachism / knowledge / experience
Basic principles of this world.

Jason DeZurik

*   *   *

Consider it pure joy, my brothers, whenever you face trials of many kinds, because you know that the testing of your faith develops perseverance.
James 1:2-3

*   *   *

Steadfastness in doing something despite difficulty or delay in achieving success.
Determination.
Patience.
endurance.
Commitment.
Application,

Jason DeZurik

Chapter 9

Prove it!

The important thing is not to stop questioning. Curiosity has its own reason for existing. One cannot help but be in awe when he contemplates the mysteries of eternity, of life, of the marvelous structure of reality. It is enough if one tries merely to comprehend a little of this mystery every day. Never lose a holy curiosity.
Albert Einstein

As he neared Damascus on his journey, suddenly a light from heaven flashed around him.
Acts 9:3

*B*efore I came into a personal relationship with Jesus Christ, my struggle in Seattle continued as I began not only to read the Bible and other books, but I also kept seeking out others who were against God and the Bible to see what they thought. I asked what conclusions they had come to about life. Now I know what was happening to me back then, but at the time I did not realize it because I had opened myself up to the idea of following truth wherever it would lead me. I had inadvertently opened myself up to Jesus Christ no matter where He would lead me. What do

I mean by this? I did not understand that in opening myself up to truth I was really opening myself up to the Creator of the universe, Jesus Christ. I did not understand this until after I became a follower of Christ. If Jesus is truth as He claimed in John 14:6, and if not everything has been written about Him as is the claim in John 21:25, then whenever I encountered truth I was directly encountering the truth of the God of the Bible. When I would encounter false teaching and lies I would almost instantly know in my spirit (even though I didn't believe I had a spirit at the time) that it was false. There are greater things afoot than we even realize.

Because I had opened myself up to seeking truth, I would know in my spirit when I came upon a false teacher who would sometimes teach truth and other times teach lies. With a false teacher, a lot of the time I would leave confused and unsettled in my spirit. When I would talk with my friend Danny Castro and listen to what he said, I would leave fulfilled and not confused. I continued to search and seek out truth for about four months. Finally I decided to call out to God with my words. I'd walk the streets of Seattle for hours talking, screaming, and listening. No one answered. Not God. Not my friends and surely not the strangers walking the streets who looked at me as if I were possessed. Boy, I'd love to know what some people were thinking while watching me.

While roaming the streets I would speak to God directly pleading:

"God, if you're real, prove yourself to me!"

"God, if you show me you are real I promise to serve you all the days of my life no questions asked."

"JESUS! WHERE THE #&@^ ARE YOU? IF YOU'RE REAL PROVE IT YOU ^*& #* @* !*%."

I was as real and as raw as could be. I wanted answers. If God was real I wanted to know. If He wasn't, I wanted to know. I promised Him if He would prove Himself to me that I would serve Him all the days of my life.

I finally got an answer. I want to be very clear on this point. I was not drunk or high or delirious in anyway when all of what I am about to tell you happened. I was stone cold sober and in a right mind when this happened.

It was very early in the morning and I was sleeping in my bed lying on my back. I awoke at 4:00a.m. I know this because I looked at my bright red digital alarm clock and saw the time. I remember this like it was yesterday, and I am still in awe at what took place. While lying there, I just sensed a presence in the room. This presence filled the entire room every nook and cranny as well as any corners and any holes that were in the room. I wasn't terrified or scared, but I had what I would call a respectful fear for what ever this was. It was like having a fearful respect for a good earthly parent -- especially a father.

I couldn't move or speak. This presence filled the room.

Then some strange things happened. I felt physical pressure on my chest and thighs. Again, I was not scared, but I had respect for this presence. Then I heard with my ears one word: "Minnesota." I knew what this meant, and I knew who this was. It was God, or a representative for God, telling me to move back to the state where I had grown up as a child -- Minnesota.

Then, the presence was gone.

That morning I called my mother and told her what had happened. She started to cry and said, "Oh Jason we are so happy for you." And I said, "You believe me?!"
My mom said, "Yes Jason, we have been praying for you for so long."

I could hardly contain myself. I realized at that moment even though I had been very selfish and thought life was all about me, my mom, dad, and sister had never given up on me and they loved me unconditionally. It was pretty amazing.

Many Christians and non-Christians alike seem to deliberately forget that at the beginning of time everything was perfect. This means that there was no death, disease, or dying. Things were very different from the world we live in today. If sin caused us to begin to die, then what other things were very different from the creation we live in today? It's as if many of us are deliberately forgetting what was written in II Peter 3:3-7:

First of all, you must understand that in the
last days scoffers will come, scoffing and
following their own evil desires. They will
say, "Where is this 'coming' he promised?
Ever since our fathers died, everything goes
on as it has since the beginning of creation."
But they deliberately forget that long ago by
God's word the heavens existed and the
earth was formed out of water and by
water. By these waters also the world of
that time was deluged and destroyed. By
the same word the present heavens and
earth are reserved for fire, being kept for the
day of judgment and destruction of
ungodly men.

It also seems that when it comes to this subject of the
beginning of time we just put logic aside and believe
whatever we're told by the so-called "experts." I have been
blessed to have time to study and to search for truth
regarding God's word and other people's take on the
natural world. I have also had many conversations with
people from all walks of life, including Christians, atheists,
agnostics, Buddhists, new age believers, deists, and many
others. It's actually pretty interesting, challenging, and
faith-building to be able to do this. One thing that seems
to come up a lot is people's belief or lack of belief in the
Bible as a whole, but particularly the beginning of the Bible
and then even in the existence of Jesus Christ. Yes, people
question His existence, even though many secular and
people of non-Christian religious beliefs have no problem

admitting that Jesus existed.

One thing that really seems to be a stumbling block for so many is what the Bible teaches about the creation of the universe. Believers and non-believers alike want to say that the Biblical account of creation cannot be real and that in no way could the universe have been created in six earth days as written about in Genesis 1. Well, what if God told us He did it in six earth days in another place in the Bible?

I know some of you reading this are probably wanting to put this down right now, but I would ask you to please hang with me until at least to the end of this chapter. I also am pretty sure some of you are thinking, something like, "Wait a minute! There are two creation stories in Genesis."

You would be correct and Appendix 2 deals with this concern. Right now, I'd like to focus in on a different place in the Bible that it talks about the days of creation being six literal earth days. Yes, I can easily make the claim "literal earth days." Why? Well, let's answer those questions from earlier in this book first. My answers are based off of Scripture, as well as logic, faith, and reason. (You can find Scripture verses in Appendix 1 to verify these.)

#1 Can the Bible be Trusted? *Yes, through much study, experience, and learning I have come to the conclusion that the Bible not only can be trusted, but it is the Word of God.*

#2 Is the God of the Bible good? *Yes, He is good and loving.*

#3 If the God of the Bible is so good and powerful, why is there death in the world? *At the beginning of time there was no death. After Adam disobeyed God and sinned is when all of creation received the consequence to that action which was death.*

#4 Is the God of the Bible perfect? *Yes, He is holy and cannot be with sin. For now the Father God must be separated from us because of our sin nature.*

#5 Can the God of the Bible lie? *No, He is perfect and holy. So, not only can He not lie but He cannot sin at all.*

#6 What does the word holy mean? *Holy means to be perfect and must be separated from sin, or without sin.*

#7 Is the God of the Bible holy? *Yes. This is why what He did through Jesus Christ was so amazing.*

#8 Is God inside or outside of time? Or both? *The God of the Bible is outside of time but can be inside of time as well. The answer is both.*

So, the God of the Bible can be trusted, He is good and perfect, He cannot lie, He is holy and he is inside and outside of time. (I encourage you to read Appendix 1 to see the Scriptural basis to back up the points above.) If you are with me on those eight points above, would you believe the God of the Bible if he told us that He made everything in the universe in six literal earth days while He was in our time? Remember, the God of the Bible cannot lie. He wrote this down Himself in what is considered one of the most influential pieces of literature of all time.

Remember that God wrote the ten commandments with His very own finger. Deuteronomy 9:10 states the following:

> The LORD gave me two stone tablets inscribed by the finger of God. On them were all the Commandments the LORD proclaimed to you on the mountain out of the fire, on the day of the assembly.

So the God of the Bible, who created the universe, also wrote the ten commandments. He wrote these while He was inside of our time on Mount Sinai. In these commandments He wrote something very interesting.

In Exodus 20:11, while telling us why we should keep the Sabbath day and rest on this day, the Lord wrote the following text: "For in six days the LORD made the heavens and the earth, the sea, and all that is in them, but he rested on the seventh day. Therefore the LORD blessed the Sabbath day and made it holy."

Did you see it?

God, while inside of our time, while our time was moving, made a remarkable claim! When He gave us these commandments the human race knew what a day already was for sure because the earth was already rotating on its axis and was in its rotation around the sun. So human beings KNEW what a day was back then.

God wrote, "For in six days the LORD made the heavens and the earth, the sea, and all that is in them, but he rested on the seventh day."

For me personally, it was so freeing and life-giving when I finally realized this that I was just beyond excited to share this with every Christ-follower on the planet. Surely, anyone who called himself or herself a Christ-follower would be just as ecstatic and excited as I was about this new found information. Right?

Well . . . not exactly.

I was shocked to find out that many people who claim to be followers of Christ were not excited at all about this information. Many said, "Well, that's nice; but science has proven that to be false." Or, "All that matters is Jesus; the beginning doesn't really matter." I had heard this all before. And friend, if you believe or feel this way, then I have some questions for you.

- Why do we wear clothes?

- Who instituted marriage between a man and a woman?

- How do we know why Jesus came to earth?

- Why are there rainbows, and they are a reminder of what promise?

- Why do we work?

All of these answers can be found in Genesis 1 – 11. The problem lies in that we as Christians get tongue-tied and cannot answer these questions because many of us do not believe the Bible from the beginning.

This is a huge issue in learning to be consistent. If we are called to be witnesses to the world for Christ, then how do we do that if we don't even believe the book that we say we follow? Or are we just fooling ourselves, and many of us really aren't Christ-followers; we just call ourselves that?

Harsh?!

Arrogant?!

I really don't think so. I believe it's the truth in love. I am warning you out of the love I have for you, my friend. Jesus talks about this in <u>Matthew 6:21</u>:

> Not everyone who says to me, 'Lord, Lord,' will enter the kingdom of heaven, but only he who does the will of my Father who is in heaven.

Are you doing God's will, or your own will? *My own. But how do I know his will for me?*

I encourage you to get on your knees and pray in your room with just you and God. If your spouse is a Christian, then nicely ask your husband or wife to pray with you and then go in a quiet place, get on your knees and pray regardless of their answer. If you are wondering, "Why should I get on my knees to pray? Is that really important?" You do not need to get on your knees. There is not a requirement to do this but I do recommend it. My wife and I were led by the Holy Spirit to begin praying together daily on our knees in the year 2010 and I can tell you there is something to it. I am not implying that it will save you or make you more holy or anything like that but it has helped us to be more submissive to God and His leading in our lives. I can just tell you that our relationship with God has grown even more by us being willing to submit to God even with our physical bodies.

I encourage you to be open to being wrong about some things. Be open to God revealing new things to you and confirming other things. Remember that God is all truth. Ask Him to lead you to truth and be willing to hear God's voice and obey.

Please pray right now.

*   *   *

In the next chapter you will read about what it means to listen to the voice of God and obey His leading through Scripture, prayer, and even listen when He speaks through other people.

When being consistent with Scripture, you must be willing to at least question what you think to be true and even be willing to be wrong if you are shown that

Scripture says something other than you have been taught as true. Let me be clear and put to bed something early on here. We always need to love. We must wrap up what we believe and how we live in love. If the Bible clearly teaches something to be a sin and it is not strictly a cultural thing for the Hebrews in biblical times back then, as revealed through proper biblical interpretation, that would be sin. We must speak the truth, still in love though. There are times we should not enable, for this is something very different, and I would say even hateful. We need to learn love and do this with the truth. **Truth and love go hand in hand. Now, go pray to the God of the universe.**

*　　*　　*

Perseverance must finish its work so that you may
be mature and complete, not lacking anything.
James 1:4

*　　*　　*

Jason DeZurik

Chapter 10

A New Beginning

See to it that no one takes you captive through hollow and deceptive philosophy, which depends on human tradition and the basic principles of this world rather than on Christ.
Apostle Paul / Colossians 2:8

If anyone considers himself religious and yet does not keep a tight rein on his tongue, he deceives himself and his religion is worthless. Religion that God our Father accepts as pure and faultless is this: to look after orphans and widows in their distress and to keep oneself from being polluted by the world.
James 1:26-27

Are you hearing God's voice correctly? There's only one way to really know the answer to that question; you must know God's Word. You must be willing to not only read God's Word, but you also must be willing to allow the Holy Spirit to speak in and through you while you are reading the Bible. Then, you must be willing to then put it into practice.

One thing that is so great about the Bible is that it is just brutally honest. Literally, I have heard so many people, believers and non-believers alike, struggle with the Bible because of things like the following thoughts:

- The Bible has so much killing, so how can it be a good book from which to get morals from?

- The God of the Bible is just power hungry. What gives Him the right to wipe people off the face of the earth anyway?

- The Israelites killed their own children. Does that mean we should do the same?

Some of you reading this know what I am talking about. Still others of you though I'm guessing are probably saying the following, "They are just lost and need their eyes opened to the truth," or, "God will deal with them." I used to think this way and I've heard others say these things too. Friends, that is not only being spiritually lazy but intellectually lazy as well. We have got to have answers to these questions because the list of questions like those above will just keep coming and coming and coming. We are to reach out! So, do it already! Or are you scared because you don't know the answers? Then GET the answers, friends. We are commanded to do so in Matthew 28:18-20:

> Then Jesus came to them and said, "All authority in heaven and on earth has been given to me. Therefore go and make disciples of all nations, baptizing them in the name of the Father and of the Son and of the Holy Spirit, and teaching them to obey

everything I have commanded you. And surely I am with you always, to the very end of the age."

We are called to live our lives in such a way that people notice Christ living in us. We are to live godly lives directed by the Holy Spirit. When we do this and become actual followers of Jesus Christ through our actions we will be able to be used by God to lead others to Him. As is written in I Corinthians 9:19-23:

> Though I am free and belong to no man, I make myself a slave to everyone, to win as many as possible. To the Jews I became like a Jew, to win the Jews. To those under the law I became like one under the law (though I myself am not under the law), so as to win those under the law. To those not having the law I became like one not having the law (though I am not free from God's law but am under Christ's law), so as to win those not having the law. To the weak I became weak, to win the weak. I have become all things to all men so that by all possible means I might save some. I do all this for the sake of the gospel, that I may share in its blessings.

Unless you really seek out truth and allow the Holy Spirit to reveal the truth to you, some of these preceding questions that people struggle with may seem like legit questions. If you have not been reading the Bible as well as asking the Holy Spirit for guidance some of these questions might be very difficult to answer. The truth of the matter is they are legitimate questions, but they are actually very simple to answer. Let's remember that the Bible is not just a book to read; you can take things away from it and then live it out. I cannot fully comprehend it, but the Bible is alive. It says so in Hebrews 4:12:

> For the word of God is living and active.
> Sharper than any double-edged sword, it
> penetrates even to dividing soul and spirit,
> joints and marrow; it judges the thoughts
> and attitudes of the heart.

Keep in mind as well that as Christ-followers, it is the job of the Holy Spirit to bring people into a right relationship with Jesus Christ. All we can do is be faithful in speaking out and living out the truth in love.

Let's take a quick look at why some of those horrible tragedies might be in the Bible. It really does all go back to the beginning.

It's a God-given right for all humans to have free will. Depending on how you view the issue, this could be a curse or a blessing. In the Garden of Eden, just after the creation of the universe, Adam and Eve were given free will. They had total freedom to do whatever they wanted. They even had freedom to go against God and His good and right ways. God showed true love by giving them this freedom. If He had created them to have no choice but to do His will, He would have been nothing but a God of tyranny. If He would have given them choice without consequences to learn from their mistakes, there would have been no reason to confess and repent from sinful ways. Since humans are the descendants of Adam and Eve we also have this sin nature that they have passed down to us. Without benefits and consequences, the natural law that God put into place, for our decisions and actions, we would not mature and many of us would stay in spiritual infancy.

However, in His infinite wisdom, He allowed the first people who represented all of humankind to choose whether they would love Him or not. They chose to defy Him. As a result, the human race today suffers the consequences of physical, mental, and spiritual death, a product of their sin and ours.

God wants us to love Him freely and on our own accord. We have the choice of following Him or not. I once heard a pastor say, "God is a gentleman. He will not force Himself on you. He will wait patiently for you to turn to Him." There is such truth in that statement.

I believe we are living in a crucial time in the United States today. In my opinion, many people want to return to a slave-like state, much like the Israelites wanted to return to slavery in Egypt after escaping it on their way to the Promised Land. Many of them were hungry and uncomfortable. They believed that living in Egypt as a slave with a full belly and some shelter was better than living freely in the desert, not knowing where they were going to stay for the night, let alone what they were going to eat the next day. But they were free. Some wanted to trade in that freedom for the security of being under very cruel slave masters who not only would tell them what to do for the day, but would punish them if they did not obey or did a poor job. I believe we are quickly rolling down this path today and soon we will have some very hard decisions to make. Will you choose liberty with little security except in our Lord, or will you choose safety and security while putting your faith and trust in men? The choice is yours.

In a nutshell, Adam and Eve trusted and respected their own thought (trust in humans) more than God. They trusted themselves more than the God of the universe that created everything. They trusted themselves more than the God who could and would supply their needs every day if they only trusted Him. Fortunately, even if they didn't trust Him, He still supplied their needs.

The same principle is true for you: <u>Even if you don't trust or obey God, He still supplies your needs</u>. Consider these examples of His provision: *Providing | Supplying*

- You have air to breathe.

- You are able to read or hear this text being read right now.

- You are able to eat daily

- You may not have the new designer clothing but we live in a society where you do not need to go without clothing. You are clothed.

These are just a few needs that He provides, not to mention all the extra non-essential things with which He also blesses you.

Some of you might be wondering what I meant earlier when I said that we are moving to a slave-like state. (I would say some of you are already there and may not even know it.) Here are just a few examples of how we place ourselves into a form of slavery:

- Living outside of your means and going into debt because you want to have something to please your flesh.

- Not taking responsibility for our own actions and putting our integrity into question. Some of us have blasted our integrity so badly that even non-Christians don't believe our testimony anymore. For some of us, our witness is giving God a bad name, and it needs to stop. What is one way to stop? We need to actually read God's Word and humbly obey the leading of the Holy Spirit.

- Being forced by the federal government to pay for programs and things with which we disagree. (I'm not simply talking about the current administration either. We have been slowly numbed into this state of slavery under the guise of it being good and secure.)

There is hope! Start living for Christ today. You have the freedom to make today a new day! That is how much God loves you. If you have accepted Jesus Christ as your Savior, you are a new creation in Christ, and it is time to start living a new life. In II Corinthians 5:17, we read, "Therefore, if anyone is in Christ, he is a new creation; the old has gone, the new has come." As Christ followers, we need to embrace this text and not only believe it to be true, but actually put our faith into action.

John Wooden, one of the greatest basketball coaches, if not the greatest coach of all time, put it this way: "Make today your masterpiece." He's right, you know. You have free will given to you by God to choose not only what to do but how you will react to trials and adversity in your life. My good friend Shane Adams, who is also a basketball coach, puts it another way, "Make Today Great!" All this means is to hear the voice of God and obey. As it says in James 4:17, "Anyone, then, who knows the good he ought to do and doesn't do it, sins."

If you are stuck in bondage and have given yourself up sexually, or you are in chains of debt or insecurity, or you have doubt wrapped around you, seek the Holy Spirit. The Spirit will direct you, but you must be willing to obey the Spirit's guidance. I also encourage you to find a brother or sister in Christ with whom you can share your praises and struggles. Find someone that you trust and respect in the Lord.

Remember: God is God. We are not. People will usually let you down, but God is always faithful. Lean on Him and His wisdom. Choose today to love and follow Him.

Have you thanked the Lord lately for His many blessings? Maybe it's time for you to confess and repent of some things in your life, stop being selfish, and give thanks for His provision and your freedom in Christ. I know II Chronicles 7:14 was meant for Israel but if we put this principle into practice today who's to say this won't happen? It says:

> If my people, who are called by my name, will humble themselves and pray and seek my face and turn from their wicked ways, then will I hear from heaven and will forgive their sin and will heal their land.

Christians, if we humble ourselves, pray, seek God's face, turn from our wicked ways, and stop living on the fence, then maybe, just maybe the Lord God of heaven will hear us and not only forgive our sin but heal our land as well. Just a thought.

* * *

For further study, read
the account of the Israelites and their
doubt of God's provision in Exodus 16:1–17:7.

Jason DeZurik

Chapter 11

We Are in a Spiritual Battle

For our struggle is not against flesh and blood,
but against the rulers, against the authorities, against
the powers of this dark world and against the
spiritual forces of evil in the heavenly realms.
Ephesians 6:12

Nobody ever defended anything successfully; there is only attack
and attack and attack some more.
General George S. Patton Jr.

When I first came across the above Patton quote, I was very excited because it expresses the method that I believe we as Christ-followers need to adopt in advancing the Kingdom of God in the spiritual realm. When Christ was tempted by Satan in the wilderness for forty days, how did Jesus engage him? Satan took God's Word out of context, and Jesus engaged him with the correct interpretation and context of the Word of God. This is what we need to do as well. We need to go on the offensive and speak the truth.

We have been in defensive mode for so long that I think we have almost forgotten how to attack Satan and his demons. Let's just face the facts: many of us who claim to be Christians have gotten lazy and expect others to take up the mantle of Christ. We need to stop reacting to what the world has to say — we need to act!

One major hurdle that we must jump over is the poor teaching from some people in the church's pulpits and leadership. Harsh? Maybe, but many of you reading this know it's true. Why can I say this so confidently? It's because I am engaged with pastors and leaders in the church every month who compromise the Word of God and do not take a stand for truth. They let the wisdom of men rule their thoughts and teachings. These heresies are then passed on to their flock. Compromise seems to have become the truth of the day. If you think I'm out in left field, please consider the following people I have personally had discussions with on this matter:

- A person who claims to follow Christ, yet says the act of homosexuality is not a sin. She believes that homosexuals should still marry even when I pointed out to her that Jesus states in Matthew 19 that marriage is between one man and one woman. Not to mention all the other places in Scripture going back even to the book of Genesis.

- A United Methodist pastor who teaches that the abortion debate is only a women's issue, so men need to take a back seat and not speak up.

- A Lutheran pastor who not only got a divorce from his wife and then was immediately let back into the pulpit with not even a thought from leadership of letting this pastor take time to heal from this wound.

- A person that claims to be a follower of Christ and helps out with church teaching events like summer Bible school who not only denies Genesis 1 – 11 as history but also denies many of the miracles in the Bible.

With these examples and so many more like them is it any wonder why the church, let alone our world, is so messed up? Is it any wonder why the world calls Christ-followers hypocrites?

Regardless of what happens in this world, our hope needs to be in Jesus Christ — not in people.

Unfortunately, we so often put our hope in people and in a politically correct mindset. We allow a comfortable mind-set to rule the day, when the truth of the matter is we need to stand up for truth in love. What comes to my mind is a vote in the Evangelical Lutheran Church of America (ELCA) in 2009 allowing practicing homosexuals to be ordained as pastors. This principle can be supported nowhere in Scripture. Even the ELCA knows something is amiss, as is evidenced by their very own actions. Why can

I make such a bold statement? Because people who are in heterosexual relationships and that are living together outside of marriage who practice sexual relations cannot be ordained in the ELCA. They know that acting on this heterosexual sexual relationship is a sin.

I believe that we have allowed sin to creep into the church, and now we don't know what we believe. First Timothy 3:1-12 shows us what kind of people should be in leadership in the church. We have bent this Scripture to the breaking point; until we are willing to rectify this problem, we will be nothing but hypocrites in the world's eyes.

> Here is a trustworthy saying: If anyone sets his heart on being an overseer, he desires a noble task. Now the overseer must be above reproach, the husband of but one wife, temperate, self-controlled, respectable, hospitable, able to teach, not given to drunkenness, not violent but gentle, not quarrelsome, not a lover of money. He must manage his own family well and see that his children obey him with proper respect. (If anyone does not know how to manage his own family, how can he take care of God's church?) He must not be a recent convert, or he may become conceited and fall under the same judgment as the devil. He must also have a good reputation with outsiders,

so that he will not fall into disgrace and into the devil's trap.

Deacons, likewise, are to be men worthy of respect, sincere, not indulging in much wine, and not pursuing dishonest gain. They must keep hold of the deep truths of the faith with a clear conscience. They must first be tested; and then if there is nothing against them, let them serve as deacons.

In the same way, their wives are to be women worthy of respect, not malicious talkers but temperate and trustworthy in everything.

A deacon must be the husband of but one wife and must manage his children and his household well.

I know this won't be popular, but many congregations have put people who aren't ready to lead into church leadership. Have the leaders in these congregations really looked at Scriptures like these to make sure these people are ready for such positions?

Each one of us who is a follower of Jesus Christ needs to live as though we believe what the Bible says — even when acting upon Scripture is the difficult thing to do. Until people see that a relationship with Jesus Christ actually works in the real world, many won't want to come to Him.

I learned the following from my good friend, Shane
Adams, who has spoken for Worldview Warriors
occasionally and coaches a high school boys' basketball
team. He teaches his team, "Play defense, and that defense
wins championships!" This sounds a little different from
the Patton quote at the beginning of this chapter until you
realize what he means by this. Before he started coaching
his new team, Shane told me, "We are going to be the most
disciplined team on the floor. We are going to slow the
game down and play defense. When we are on offense, we
will control the ball until a great shot opens up."

Do you see the wisdom in this philosophy? Stay on the
offense, attack, attack, and attack some more. The best
defense you can have is a strong offense that looks for the
great opportunity to score — not a good opportunity, but a
great opportunity. With this comes patience and discipline.

How many of us reading this book right now look at
discipline as a bad thing? We need to understand that
discipline is a good thing. It is meant to help us mature
and not be infants, toddlers, or adolescents mentally and
spiritually anymore. James 1:2-4 says:

> Consider it pure joy my brothers and sisters
> whenever you face trials of many kinds,
> because you know that the testing of your
> faith develops perseverance. Perseverance

> must finish its work so that you may be
> mature and complete, not lacking anything.

Discipline is not just getting a bad consequence for some action you or I have done. It is also what we can receive once we know how to respond to the Word of the Lord and His leading. Discipline can be a very good thing. For instance, we are disciplined to obey His leading and not to go our own way because we know that by going against God there will be consequences to our actions. In the same way we can receive good benefits for going God's way.

Our six children consist of two boys and four girls. We have taught all of our children two main things in our home:

#1 Do not lie. Once you lose people's trust with your words it is very difficult to be taken seriously by anyone.

#2 Obey God. Since God has put us as parents over you, obey your parents.

That's pretty much it. If they do not follow these simple rules they receive a consequence or discipline for their action. And as stated earlier in this book we require first time obedience. This is so important. Yes, this can be very difficult and tiring for parents, but it is so important for children in order for them to feel safe and secure. I can tell you that when my wife and I get lazy and do not require first time obedience is when chaos starts to rear its ugly head in our house along with insecurity. Put another way, when my wife and I take time to teach discipline in our home, our house is then in order and at peace. All of us then live disciplined lives.

Our two sons are only fifteen months apart. When they were toddlers, people would always ask us if they were twins. That is how much they looked alike to people when they were younger. Even though they act alike in many ways they are very different people in so many other ways. One way they are very different is how we needed to train them regarding obedience in order to live disciplined lives.

As little boys, our oldest understood about the line we "drew in the sand" for him with our simple rules and he knew not to cross it. He knew if he did cross the line he would be disciplined by us and receive a consequence for his actions. It was fairly easy to know when he should receive a consequence for his actions. Just when my wife and I thought we had it all figured out, our second son came along and was completely different.

For instance, if my wife would wash the kitchen floor and told the boys not to go in the kitchen until she said it was okay, we would have two very different reactions. Ezra, our oldest, would either obey or disobey. He would either stay out of the kitchen, and sometimes even stay out of the room next to the kitchen, or he might make the kitchen his own personal slip and slide. As a parent this made it pretty easy to know when he was obeying or disobeying in that circumstance. Elijah, our second born son, was very different. Not only would he stay in the room next to the kitchen but he would stand as close to the kitchen as he could looking in and being right on the edge of possibly being in the kitchen without going into it. Now this was completely foreign to us. What should we do? Well, thanks to a wonderful resource that my wife and I highly recommend, called _Growing Kids God's Way_ by Gary and Sue Ezzo, we were able to realize that Elijah had an issue of the "heart" that we needed to deal with. He had a sinful bent to push the boundaries that, as his parents, we needed to help him through.

Ezra, our oldest, is very justice oriented. Elijah, our second son, is pretty carefree. Ezra is very aware of boundaries - his own as well as others' - which can lead to very interesting discussions at home. When Elijah was younger, he was a much more "outside the lines" kind of a guy, not in a bad way but in a way that would push the boundary and make you, as a parent, question if he might be sinning or not.

What matters in this circumstance is the "heart". If the intent is to see how much you can get away with then you have an issue with obeying and doing what God wants you to do. You probably want to serve yourself and not God. If your intent is to please God then that will show too.

We now see how much Elijah wants to serve God in all that he does. At a young age he was just very curious, and he was always testing us to see if we would follow through in what we said. Now that he is older and we did the difficult thing in disciplining him when he was younger, Elijah is a big jokester, who is very good at strategies in games and in life. Since we were able to help him hone this gift from God to be used for good and not evil, his desire now is to be used by God in everything.

Christians, aren't you tired of living for yourself? Our faith is found in Jesus Christ and no other. Let's start living what the Bible teaches us to believe so the world can see the truth. This will not be easy, but if you are in the center of God's will, you will have peace of mind. If you want safety, then please stop following Jesus and claiming to be His follower. You are giving Him and His followers a bad name. Being in the center of God's will is not safe, but it is an adventure! ✸

We need to learn truth and have a solid biblical foundation set in Christ. We need to be disciplined with our relationship with Jesus Christ. We not only need to speak the truth in love, but we also need to show truth through our actions as well. As Christ-followers we need to engage people right where they are in the culture. Remember that people who are blinded by false teachings are not the enemy; Satan and his demons are the enemy. We need to speak and act in love toward people.

This book is meant to equip the saints, adults and students alike, to not only know what we believe and why we believe it, but also to be on the offensive and attacking the enemy's lies.

*   *   *

Do you agree that discipline can be a good thing or not? Why do you think that way? Back up your belief with Scripture.

Let the following Scripture passages encourage you in learning more about discipline:

Job 5:17 - Proverbs 19:20 - II Timothy 1:17
Revelation 3:18-20 - Jeremiah 1:5
Jeremiah 29:11 - Genesis 1:26-31

Zealous
↓
Devoted
Committed
Dedicated
Passionate

Repent
↓
feel or express sincere regret or remorse about one's wrong doing or sin.

Jason DeZurik

*   *   *

Those who would give up essential liberty
to purchase a little temporary safety
deserve neither liberty nor safety.
Benjamin Franklin

*   *   *

Jason DeZurik

Chapter 12

Doing The Right Thing

Trust in the Lord with all your heart and lean not on your own understanding; in all your ways acknowledge him, and he will make your paths straight.
Proverbs 3:5–6

My concern is not whether God is on our side; my greatest concern is to be on God's side, for God is always right.
Abraham Lincoln

𝒟*ear* Mr. DeZurik,

I wanted to apologize to you. I opened an (account with a social networking site) without my parents' permission and lied about my age. Then I asked you to be my friend. I was wrong to do this. I will be closing the account and not opening one again until I am old enough.
Sincerely,
(Young Person's Name)

I received the above note from a young man who was learning a hard lesson — how to be a man of integrity. He was learning how to be godly even though it is difficult.

It was such a blessing for me to receive the note and apology from this young man in person. Most likely it was uncomfortable for him because he did not know what my reaction would be. I forgave him and encouraged him to become the man of God he is called to be.

I'm encouraged by having friends like his parents who, like my wife and me, are trying to raise godly children. It is not easy to admit when you're wrong or to teach your child to take the difficult road (the "narrow path"), but God has called us to this kind of living. In the long run, taking the narrow road will reap rewards in your life, your child's life, and society as a whole.

As children of the most high King, we must not only teach God's ways, but also live His ways in order for people to understand the life that He offers. We must live for our King and not for our own selfish, evil desires. The carnal (Flesh) must die, and God must increase in our lives.

One of the students to whom we ministered during one of our speaking tours through the southwestern United States said the following, "I love the way y'all say things without hesitating. You aren't afraid to speak the truth, even if it hurts or is embarrassing. I think that a lot of people today don't want to stand up for this kind of thing,"

He also said that many people today appear to worship God in church and during religious activities, but then they go home and engage in immoral activities on their own time. This student even wondered if these people are actually Christians. It was obviously upsetting to him.

It makes me think again of Matthew 7:13-14, when Jesus says:

> Enter through the narrow gate. For wide is the gate and broad is the road that leads to destruction and many enter through it. But small is the gate and narrow the road that leads to life and only a few find it.

Yes, the gate to life is narrow, but I think we tend to forget that the road to life is also narrow. We cannot simply pray a prayer and then leave it at that. We must repent and turn from our wicked ways. This is where it gets tough.

Years ago, I had a very difficult situation arise with a good friend who claimed to be a Christian and even was in ministry with me for a while. One day, however, I caught him in a lie, followed by more lies. I confronted him about his dishonesty. He admitted that he had lied not only once, but also numerous times before that. I forgave him, and we moved on. Later I caught him in more lies, so I asked another brother in Christ to accompany me when I confronted this man. He again admitted his guilt. I told him that I forgave him and that we would just move on from that point. All was forgiven; however, I told him, "Always tell me the truth from this point on, even if it is very difficult to do so." We continued our friendship as if the lying had never taken place. This peace lasted about one month, until I sensed that he was lying again. I confronted him about it again, but this time he grew defensive and stated that I was just paranoid. He began to ignore me and failed to return my phone calls or e-mails.

This totally confused me because I thought that we had moved on from these lies.

Obviously, he was continuing his path of lies. However, he no longer seemed remorseful about his actions. Thus, I had to deal with a very difficult situation and make some hard decisions.

I believe that a biblical worldview holds that a person who sins and is not willing to turn from their wicked ways should not be in leadership in the church. At this point, I am not talking about a person who has confessed their sins, repented, and received healing or is at least truly striving to be healed. Other people saw my friend's hypocrisy in action, and I had to attempt to mend the bridge in those relationships. This went even up to the point of dealing with a financial bill that he said was taken care of almost four years before, and I had to deal with it four years later and make it right. You see, as Christ-followers we must always live above reproach admitting a wrong even years later not only for our healing, but for the healing of others. I share this story with you because at that time I was also questioning whether my friend was even a Christian. I asked God and myself, "How can he be a Christian when he is definitely not walking the narrow path as Jesus Christ has told us to do?" I was consumed with this situation and bewildered over how it could be happening.

I do not write this to condemn, but to challenge each and every Christian. Live out your faith in Christ! First Corinthians 15 is a great passage to read about actually living out our faith in Jesus Christ and His life, death, and resurrection. We need to live it out in our actions, not just with our words.

After much prayer, meditation, and counsel from wise brothers in Christ, God freed me from this situation. Praise God that He allowed me to think this through and see clearly. I forgave my friend and tried to make things right with him as Jesus taught, even though I was wronged. However, because my friend did not like what I believe are the God-given standards by which we are to live, we don't talk at all anymore. It is sad, but probably a good thing. Praise God that my family and I are now free to do what God has called us to do. I don't need to worry anymore whether this person is telling the truth or is lying again. My family and I now focus on Christ.

God is the judge — not us. It is up to Him as to who is following the narrow path and entering through the narrow gate. The burden is on Him, not you or me. Later Jesus says in Matthew 7:21-23:

> Not everyone who says to me, 'Lord, Lord,'
> will enter the kingdom of heaven, but only
> he who does the will of my Father who is in
> heaven. Many will say to me on that day,
> 'Lord, Lord, did we not prophesy in your
> name, and in your name drive out demons
> and perform many miracles?' Then I will
> tell them plainly, 'I never knew you. Away
> from me, you evildoers!'

So, the question each one of us needs to answer and examine in our own life is this: Am I truly willing to follow Christ in everything I do, not being a hypocrite?!

Seek God out, hear His voice and obey. You will not be sorry.

Desire | Find

*   *   *

For further reading, check out the scripture below and an old book by Andrew Murray called *Absolute Surrender*, and read Matthew 7:13-29.

Jason DeZurik

Appendix 1

#1 Can the Bible be trusted?

II Peter 1:16-21 - II Timothy 3:14-17

Proverbs 30:5-6

#2 Is the God of the Bible good?

Psalm 119:68 - Psalm 73:1 - Exodus 33:19

Psalm 135:3 - I Timothy 4:4

Hebrews 6:5 - Psalm 16:2

#3 If the God of the Bible is so good and powerful, why is there death in the world?

Genesis 1 - Genesis 2 - Genesis 3

[Note: In order to understand the importance of Jesus coming to earth we must understand why He came to earth.]

Is the God of the Bible perfect?
Mark 10:18 - Habakkuk 1:13

II Samuel 22:31 - Matthew 5:48

Psalm 18:30

#4 Can the God of the Bible lie at all?
Romans 3:4 - Numbers 23:19 - Titus 1:2

Hebrews 6:18 - I Samuel 15:29

#5 What does the word holy mean?
I Peter 1:13-16 - Leviticus 11:44

Leviticus 19:2 - I Peter 2:9

#6 Is the God of the Bible holy?
Isaiah 6:3 - I Samuel 2:2 - Hosea 11:9

Psalm 40:5 - Revelation 4:8 - Exodus 3:4-5

[Note: When the Bible says something three times, like "holy, holy, holy," it's called a trihagion. Repetition three

times like that is expressing that idea with as much force and passion as is possible. It expresses the supreme holiness of God. It's also significant in that it's a reflection of the triune nature of God.]

#7 Is God inside or outside of time? Or both?

Revelation 1:4 - Revelation 4:8 ("day and night")

Psalm 90 - Jude 25 - 2 Peter 3:8 - John 17:5

Genesis 1:1 - John 1:1 - Colossians 1:16

Appendix 2

Note from Jason: My friend Bill Seng will be dealing with the supposed problem of two creation stories at the beginning of Genesis. He deals with it more extensively in his book, *The World That Then Was*.

The Problem

There is an apparent problem in Genesis chapter two. This problem, according to the skeptics, is that it presents a second creation account. They say that it is not just a different perspective on the account given in chapter one, but that it is entirely unique to the first. In Genesis chapter one, there is a definite structure. First God created light, then he separated the waters, created dry land, and so forth until he finally created man and woman. But in Genesis chapter two, after the first three verses, it appears as though it returns to a world that was formless and empty.

The literalist who reads the creation account and holds the Bible as the authoritative Word of God would struggle to defend the notion that the earth was created in the order that Genesis chapter one describes. It would then become difficult to harmonize Genesis chapter one with chapter two. Are there two creation accounts in the Bible?

The Simple Solution

Despite the claim against the notion that chapters one and two are complementary it would appear to be the simplest explanation. Chapter one is a broad overview concerning how God created the earth. Chapter two is a detailed account of day six of creation. Day six is special because it was on that day God chose to form his most important creation, man.

It can be observed in chapters one and two that man was a very special creation. Man was created in the image of God! Having created man in God's image, the Holy Spirit found it necessary to expound on what it meant to be created in the image of God. Chapter two contains a beautiful narrative of how God fashioned man, taught him how to live by giving him authority over creation, and then created a "help meet" that was both suitable and desirable for him. Learning about the creation and intention of man provides valuable insights into the nature of God. And yet God is different from his creation as is revealed in the first two chapters of Genesis. In chapter one, he is untouchable in relation to his creation. He reaches out and touches his creation in chapter two.

The Sophisticated Solution

This is the account of the heavens and the

*earth when they were created. When the
LORD God made the earth and the heavens
– and no shrub of the field had yet appeared
on the earth and no plant of the field had yet
sprung up, for the LORD God had not sent
rain on the earth and there was no man to
work the ground, but streams came up from
the earth and watered the whole surface of
the ground – the LORD God formed the
man from the dust of the ground and
breathed into his nostrils the breath of life,
and the man became a living being.*[1]

One must pay close attention to the language of
the author to understand the incredible consistency
between chapters one and two of Genesis. It is easy to
overlook the intentional use of the language
describing the different types of vegetation in
chapters one and two. Vocabulary differences as
simple as the *vegetation* produced by the land in
chapter one and the *shrub of the field* and *plant of the
field* in chapter are not easily recognized by the
average reader. After digging deeper into the author's
original intent for using these specific words and
phrases can it be seen that Genesis two is an
elaboration of the creation account and not a unique
story.

---

[1] Genesis 2:4-7.

[2] John H. Sailhammer and Frank E. Gaebelein, ed., *The Expositor's*

The vegetation that God created in chapter one is different from the plants and shrubs described at the beginning of Genesis chapter two. Genesis chapters 1 and 2 establish that mankind could eat of any of the plants "on the face of the whole earth and every tree" (Genesis 1:29). After the Fall, Genesis 3:17 limits man's diet to the "plants of the field." The fields had to be planted by mankind. In light of this, the phrases "shrub of the field" and "plant of the field," in 2:5, are surprisingly descriptive in conveying the difference. These specific phrases implied that nothing of the "field" had yet grown. The vegetation God created in chapter one was not related to the fields mentioned in chapter two. In fact, it was not even related to the garden that he planted for Adam.[2]

The Rain

The reference to the rain anticipates the rain waters of the Flood. The Flood occurred long after Adam and Eve had passed away: "On that day all the springs of the great deep burst forth, and the floodgates of the heavens were opened. And rain fell on the earth forty days and forty nights" (Genesis

---

[2] John H. Sailhammer and Frank E. Gaebelein, ed., *The Expositor's Bible Commentary Vol. 2* (Grand Rapids, Michigan: Zondervan, 1990), 40-41.

7:11-12). Although it is never mentioned in Scripture, it is traditionally believed that before the Flood, there was no rainfall. Therefore, the reference to rain is probably in relation to the rain waters of the flood.[3]

Conclusion

No contradiction exists between Genesis chapters one and two. The reference to the absence of the shrubs and plants of the fields indicates that man had to work the ground to get it to produce food after the Fall. The rain that had not been sent from God referred to the total lack of rain before the flood of Noah's day and anticipated the waters of the flood. Through God's inspiration the author of Genesis was aware of the earth's situation before and after sin entered the world. The accounts in Genesis one and two can be defended both on simple and sophisticated levels to clearly show that no contradiction exists between the two and that they are two parts of one complete creation story.

---

[3] Sailhamer and Gaebelein, 40.

Jason DeZurik

*What others are saying about the ministry of
Jason DeZurik and his family
as well as Worldview Warriors*

Jason DeZurik is truly a man of God! I have known him for years and have been on the road with him on several tours. I've seen Jason grow so much in the past years and he really is a true leader. I will always stand with Jason!

Ryan Edberg
Lead Singer and Song Writer
Silverline

*   *   *

After serving in ministry with Jason DeZurik for nine years, and knowing him as a personal friend since 1997, I can say that the word 'consistent' identifies his life. You know what you are going to get from Jason every single time. You get a man who loves his Lord first and faithfully lives that out in his family and ministry. Jason does not stray from a consistent commitment to knowing and living the Word of God. He's given his life to it.

Marc Quinter
Lead Pastor
Amelia United Methodist Church
Amelia, OH

When you read Jason DeZurik's book, you will soon realize that he is a cheerleader for the Lord. His enthusiasm in reaching our young people for Christ is his calling, passion and motivation. He has traveled thousands of miles, crisscrossing the United States, speaking at Christian concerts, churches, youth groups and county fairs. He challenges our youth to accept Jesus Christ as their individual personal Savior.

Jason has a weekly Sunday night program (Do Not Keep Silent) on our network of radio stations. On this program, he challenges our youth on the current topics and events that they face on a daily basis. He gets them thinking - not only with their heads, but with their hearts, as he points them towards Biblical truth. Jason truly is a dedicated servant of the Lord.

Daniel L. Kayser
President & CEO
Kayser Broadcast Ministries, Inc.

*   *   *

I would storm the gates of Hell with Jason DeZurik with a water pistol.

Nathan Buck
Founding Pastor
The Catalyst Church
Findlay, OH

I would loved to have been there when Jason read the verse that says 'we live by faith and not by sight' for the first time. Something clicked in Jason's mind and spirit when he read that because he truly lives by it. Jason has taught me so much just by example. Some teachers teach and others live by example, but Jason DeZurik does both. I encourage you to read some of his life stories, especially the one about the milk, and strive to apply it to your own lives.

Scott Mason
Author
No Reason To Live; Beauty & Disgrace

*   *   *

Any time I have the chance to have Jason come and minister to our students I jump on it. The work that he and his team are doing is God-inspired, and for God. Their passion is to reach these students and lead them to a relationship with Jesus, whether it is a new relationship, or reigniting the fire for those who have gone away from their relationship. Jason DeZurik and his team are truly working for God in all that they do!

Justin York
Youth Pastor
Not Alone Ministries
Kewanee, IL

I have had the opportunity to work alongside Jason DeZurik on several occasions and have been absolutely blown away by each of his messages.

George Sweatt
Youth Coordinator
Family Life Network
Bath, NY

* * *

Once we met Jason DeZurik we quickly knew he was a man after God's own heart.

Aaron Collins
Bassist and Lead Vocalist
Paint the Sky Black

* * *

Jason DeZurik connects. With kids. With seekers. With listeners – all who have ears to hear. For more than a decade, I have known Jason as my children's youth pastor, as a fervent co-worker in the fields of the Lord, and as a friend. For years, Jason served faithfully as a youth leader at a large church in our small town. Our family's church didn't quite have enough youth to form any kind of group. But Jason's impassioned youth outreach drew children from most every church in town – not just for games, but for the

Gospel. He preached it straight, no compromises. And kids – mine among them – responded, because Jason had the courage to speak Truth to them – even when it was hard to hear, and even harder to obey. And we're just one family among the hundreds and thousands who already have been touched by God's grace, through this Godly man.

Jennifer Bacon Miller
Director
We Care For Students
Religious Education Ministry

*   *   *

Jason DeZurik is one of the most compassionate people I have ever met. I have really come to respect his willingness to truly listen to people. His heart to grow the kingdom of God and reach youth right where they are at is something we all can learn from!

Steve Adams
Lead Guitarist and Song Writer
Silverline

*   *   *

From the time I have spent with Jason, it is so clear and evident that he not only walks close with God, but he allows God to speak through him. Jason DeZurik is a humble yet powerful speaker. His words will stay with you and hit straight to the heart.

AJ Cheek
Musician
Nashville, TN

Equipping Students to Impact This Generation for Jesus Christ

www.worldviewwarriors.org

Worldview Warriors - P.O. Box 681
Findlay, OH 45839
Office phone: 419-310-6249
info@worldviewwarriors.org

Free weekly resources available to use in personal study,
small groups, Sunday school classes, sermons, etc.

For booking Worldview Warriors speakers,
bands, and events contact Jeff Sanders at 716-969-7352

DONOTKEEPSILENT

www.donotkeepsilent.com

Jason DeZurik's weekly 2-hour radio show

Find Worldview Warriors and
Do Not Keep Silent on Facebook and Twitter

To book Jason DeZurik for a speaking
engagement contact Last Hope Music

www.lasthopemusic.com

218-330-3988

Jason DeZurik

To find out more about the health cooperative
Jason and his family are a part of go to
www.samaritanministries.org

*If you decide to join this health cooperative
please inform Samaritan Ministries that you
were referred to them by: Jason DeZurik.*

Thank you.

NOTES:

NOTES:

NOTES:

NOTES:

NOTES:

NOTES: